W9-AUY-186

THE HISTORY & CULTURE of NATIVE AMERICANS

The Iroquois

THE HISTORY & CULTURE of NATIVE AMERICANS

THE HISTORY & CULTURE of NATIVE AMERICANS

The Iroquois

BRUCE E. JOHANSEN

Series Editor
PAUL C. ROSIER

CHELSEA HOUSE
PUBLISHERS
An imprint of Infobase Publishing

I would like to acknowledge my usual partners in the historical journey,
often Iroquois people who have shared their stories, most notably,
for this volume, Barbara Alice Mann, of Ohio, as well as
Salli Benedict and Barbara Gray (Kanatiyosh), both of Akwesasne.

The Iroquois
Copyright © 2010 by Infobase Publishing

Chelsea House
An imprint of Infobase Publishing
132 West 31st Street
New York NY 10001

Library of Congress Cataloging-in-Publication Data
Johansen, Bruce E. (Bruce Elliott), 1950–
The Iroquois / By Bruce E. Johansen.
   p. cm. — (The history and culture of native Americans)
Includes bibliographical references and index.
ISBN 978-1-60413-794-1 (hardcover)
1. Iroquois Indians—History—Juvenile literature. I. Title. II. Series.
E99.I7J64 2010
974.7004'—dc22   2010011810

Chelsea House books are available at special discounts when purchased in bulk
quantities for businesses, associations, institutions, or sales promotions. Please call
our Special Sales Department in New York at (212) 967-8800 or (800) 322-8755.

You can find Chelsea House on the World Wide Web at
http://www.chelseahouse.com

Text design by Lina Farinella
Cover design by Alicia Post
Composition by Lina Farinella
Cover printed by Bang Printing, Brainerd, Minn.
Book printed and bound by Bang Printing, Brainerd, Minn.
Date printed: September 2010
Printed in the United States of America

10 9 8 7 6 5 4 3 2 1

This book is printed on acid-free paper.

All links and Web addresses were checked and verified to be correct at the time of
publication. Because of the dynamic nature of the Web, some addresses and links
may have changed since publication and may no longer be valid.

Contents

Foreword
by Paul C. Rosier

Native American words, phrases, and tribal names are embedded in the very geography of the United States—in the names of creeks, rivers, lakes, cities, and states, including Alabama, Connecticut, Iowa, Kansas, Illinois, Missouri, Oklahoma, and many others. Yet Native Americans remain the most misunderstood ethnic group in the United States. This is a result of limited coverage of Native American history in middle schools, high schools, and colleges; poor coverage of contemporary Native American issues in the news media; and stereotypes created by Hollywood movies, sporting events, and TV shows.

Two newspaper articles about American Indians caught my eye in recent months. Paired together, they provide us with a good introduction to the experiences of American Indians today: first, how they are stereotyped and turned into commodities; and second, how they see themselves being a part of the United States and of the wider world. (Note: I use the terms *Native Americans* and *American Indians* interchangeably; both terms are considered appropriate.)

In the first article, "Humorous Souvenirs to Some, Offensive Stereotypes to Others," written by Carol Berry in *Indian Country Today*, I read that tourist shops in Colorado were selling "souvenir" T-shirts portraying American Indians as drunks. "My Indian name is Runs with Beer," read one T-shirt offered in Denver. According to the article, the T-shirts are "the kind of stereotype-reinforcing products also seen in nearby Boulder, Estes Park, and likely other Colorado communities, whether as part of the tourism trade or as everyday merchandise." No other ethnic group in the United States is stereotyped in such a public fashion. In addition, Native people are used to sell a range of consumer goods, including the

Jeep Cherokee, Red Man chewing tobacco, Land O'Lakes butter, and other items that either objectify or insult them, such as cigar store Indians. As importantly, non-Indians learn about American Indian history and culture through sports teams such as the Atlanta Braves, Cleveland Indians, Florida State Seminoles, or Washington Redskins, whose name many American Indians consider a racist insult; dictionaries define *redskin* as a "disparaging" or "offensive" term for American Indians. When fans in Atlanta do their "tomahawk chant" at Braves baseball games, they perform two inappropriate and related acts: One, they perpetuate a stereotype of American Indians as violent; and two, they tell a historical narrative that covers up the violent ways that Georgians treated the Cherokee during the Removal period of the 1830s.

The second article, written by Melissa Pinion-Whitt of the San Bernardino *Sun* addressed an important but unknown dimension of Native American societies that runs counter to the irresponsible and violent image created by products and sporting events. The article, "San Manuels Donate $1.7 M for Aid to Haiti," described a Native American community that had sent aid to Haiti after it was devastated in January 2010 by an earthquake that killed more than 200,000 people, injured hundreds of thousands more, and destroyed the Haitian capital. The San Manuel Band of Mission Indians in California donated $1.7 million to help relief efforts in Haiti; San Manuel children held fund-raisers to collect additional donations. For the San Manuel Indians it was nothing new; in 2007 they had donated $1 million to help Sudanese refugees in Darfur. San Manuel also contributed $700,000 to relief efforts following Hurricane Katrina and Hurricane Rita, and donated $1 million in 2007 for wildfire recovery in Southern California.

Such generosity is consistent with many American Indian nations' cultural practices, such as the "give-away," in which wealthy tribal members give to the needy, and the "potlatch," a winter gift-giving ceremony and feast tradition shared by tribes in the Pacific Northwest. And it is consistent with historical accounts of Ameri-

can Indians' generosity. For example, in 1847 Cherokee and Choctaw, who had recently survived their forced march on a "Trail of
Tears" from their homelands in the American South to present-
day Oklahoma, sent aid to Irish families after reading of the po-
tato famine, which created a similar forced migration of Irish. A
Cherokee newspaper editorial, quoted in Christine Kinealy's *The
Great Irish Famine: Impact, Ideology, and Rebellion*, explained that
the Cherokee "will be richly repaid by the consciousness of having done a good act, by the moral effect it will produce abroad."
During and after World War II, nine Pueblo communities in New
Mexico offered to donate food to the hungry in Europe, after Pueblo army veterans told stories of suffering they had witnessed while
serving in the United States armed forces overseas. Considering
themselves a part of the wider world, Native people have reached
beyond their borders, despite their own material poverty, to help
create a peaceful world community.

American Indian nations have demonstrated such generosity within the United States, especially in recent years. After the
terrorist attacks of September 11, 2001, the Lakota Sioux in South
Dakota offered police officers and emergency medical personnel to
New York City to help with relief efforts; Indian nations across the
country sent millions of dollars to help the victims of the attacks.
As an editorial in the *Native American Times* newspaper explained
on September 12, 2001, "American Indians love this country like
no other. . . . Today, we are all New Yorkers."

Indeed, Native Americans have sacrificed their lives in defend-
ing the United States from its enemies in order to maintain their
right to be both American and Indian. As the volumes in this series
tell us, Native Americans patriotically served as soldiers (including
as "code talkers") during World War I and World War II, as well
as during the Korean War, the Vietnam War, and, after 9/11, the
wars in Afghanistan and Iraq. Native soldiers, men and women, do
so today by the tens of thousands because they believe in America,
an America that celebrates different cultures and peoples. Sergeant

Leonard Gouge, a Muscogee Creek, explained it best in an article in *Cherokee News Path* in discussing his post-9/11 army service. He said he was willing to serve his country abroad because "by supporting the American way of life, I am preserving the Indian way of life."

This new Chelsea House series has two main goals. The first is to document the rich diversity of American Indian societies and the ways their cultural practices and traditions have evolved over time. The second goal is to provide the reader with coverage of the complex relationships that have developed between non-Indians and Indians over the past several hundred years. This history helps to explain why American Indians consider themselves both American and Indian and why they see preserving this identity as a strength of the American way of life, as evidence to the rest of the world that America is a champion of cultural diversity and religious freedom. By exploring Native Americans' cultural diversity and their contributions to the making of the United States, these volumes confront the stereotypes that paint all American Indians as the same and portray them as violent; as "drunks," as those Colorado T-shirts do; or as rich casino owners, as many news accounts do.

✳ ✳ ✳

Each of the 14 volumes in this series is written by a scholar who shares my conviction that young adult readers are both fascinated by Native American history and culture and have not been provided with sufficient material to properly understand the diverse nature of this complex history and culture. The authors themselves represent a varied group that includes university teachers and professional writers, men and women, and Native and non-Native. To tell these fascinating stories, this talented group of scholars has examined an incredible variety of sources, both the primary sources that historical actors have created and the secondary sources that historians and anthropologists have written to make sense of the past.

Although the 14 Indian nations (also called tribes and communities) selected for this series have different histories and cultures, they all share certain common experiences. In particular, they had to face an American empire that spread westward in the eighteenth and nineteenth centuries, causing great trauma and change for all Native people in the process. Because each volume documents American Indians' experiences dealing with powerful non-Indian institutions and ideas, I outline below the major periods and features of federal Indian policy-making in order to provide a frame of reference for complex processes of change with which American Indians had to contend. These periods—Assimilation, Indian New Deal, Termination, Red Power, and Self-determination—and specific acts of legislation that define them—in particular the General Allotment Act, the Indian Reorganization Act, and the Indian Self-determination and Education Assistance Act—will appear in all the volumes, especially in the latter chapters.

In 1851, the commissioner of the federal Bureau of Indian Affairs (BIA) outlined a three-part program for subduing American Indians militarily and assimilating them into the United States: concentration, domestication, and incorporation. In the first phase, the federal government waged war with the American Indian nations of the American West in order to "concentrate" them on reservations, away from expanding settlements of white Americans and immigrants. Some American Indian nations experienced terrible violence in resisting federal troops and state militia; others submitted peacefully and accepted life on a reservation. During this phase, roughly from the 1850s to the 1880s, the U.S. government signed hundreds of treaties with defeated American Indian nations. These treaties "reserved" to these American Indian nations specific territory as well as the use of natural resources. And they provided funding for the next phase of "domestication."

During the domestication phase, roughly the 1870s to the early 1900s, federal officials sought to remake American Indians in the mold of white Americans. Through the Civilization Program, which actually started with President Thomas Jefferson, federal officials sent religious missionaries, farm instructors, and teachers to the newly created reservations in an effort to "kill the Indian to save the man," to use a phrase of that time. The ultimate goal was to extinguish American Indian cultural traditions and turn American Indians into Christian yeoman farmers. The most important piece of legislation in this period was the General Allotment Act (or Dawes Act), which mandated that American Indian nations sell much of their territory to white farmers and use the proceeds to farm on what was left of their homelands. The program was a failure, for the most part, because white farmers got much of the best arable land in the process. Another important part of the domestication agenda was the federal boarding school program, which required all American Indian children to attend schools to further their rejection of Indian ways and the adoption of non-Indian ways. The goal of federal reformers, in sum, was to incorporate (or assimilate) American Indians into American society as individual citizens and not as groups with special traditions and religious practices.

During the 1930s some federal officials came to believe that American Indians deserved the right to practice their own religion and sustain their identity as Indians, arguing that such diversity made America stronger. During the Indian New Deal period of the 1930s, BIA commissioner John Collier devised the Indian Reorganization Act (IRA), which passed in 1934, to give American Indian nations more power, not less. Not all American Indians supported the IRA, but most did. They were eager to improve their reservations, which suffered from tremendous poverty that resulted in large measure from federal policies such as the General Allotment Act.

Some federal officials opposed the IRA, however, and pushed for the assimilation of American Indians in a movement called Termination. The two main goals of Termination advocates, during the 1950s and 1960s, were to end (terminate) the federal reservation system and American Indians' political sovereignty derived from treaties and to relocate American Indians from rural reservations to urban areas. These coercive federal assimilation policies in turn generated resistance from Native Americans, including young activists who helped to create the so-called Red Power era of the 1960s and 1970s, which coincided with the African-American civil rights movement. This resistance led to the federal government's rejection of Termination policies in 1970. And in 1975 the U.S. Congress passed the Indian Self-determination and Education Assistance Act, which made it the government's policy to support American Indians' right to determine the future of their communities. Congress then passed legislation to help American Indian nations to improve reservation life; these acts strengthened American Indians' religious freedom, political sovereignty, and economic opportunity.

All American Indians, especially those in the western United States, were affected in some way by the various federal policies described above. But it is important to highlight the fact that each American Indian community responded in different ways to these pressures for change, both the detribalization policies of assimilation and the retribalization policies of self-determination. There is no one group of "Indians." American Indians were and still are a very diverse group. Some embraced the assimilation programs of the federal government and rejected the old traditions; others refused to adopt non-Indian customs or did so selectively, on their own terms. Most American Indians, as I noted above, maintain a dual identity of American and Indian.

Today, there are more than 550 American Indian (and Alaska Natives) nations recognized by the federal government. They have a legal and political status similar to states, but they have special rights and privileges that are the result of congressional acts and the hundreds of treaties that still govern federal-Indian relations today. In July 2008, the total population of American Indians (and Alaska Natives) was 4.9 million, representing about 1.6 percent of the United States population. The state with the highest number of American Indians is California, followed by Oklahoma, home to the Cherokee (the largest American Indian nation in terms of population), and then Arizona, home to the Navajo (the second-largest

American Indian nation). All told, roughly half of the American Indian population lives in urban areas; the other half lives on reservations and in other rural parts of the country. Like all their fellow American citizens, American Indians pay federal taxes, obey federal laws, and vote in federal, state, and local elections; they also participate in the democratic processes of their American Indian nations, electing judges, politicians, and other civic officials.

This series on the history and culture of Native Americans celebrates their diversity and differences as well as the ways they have strengthened the broader community of America. Ronnie Lupe, the chairman of the White Mountain Apache government in Arizona, once addressed questions from non-Indians as to "why Indians serve the United States with such distinction and honor?" Lupe, a Korean War veteran, answered those questions during the Gulf War of 1991–1992, in which Native American soldiers served to protect the independence of the Kuwaiti people. He explained in "Chairman's Corner" in *The Fort Apache Scout* that "our loyalty to the United States goes beyond our need to defend our home and reservation lands. . . . Only a few in this country really understand that the indigenous people are a national treasure. Our values have the potential of creating the social, environmental, and spiritual healing that could make this country truly great."

—Paul C. Rosier
Associate Professor of History
Villanova University

Iroquois Origins
and
Ceremonial Culture

This book briefly surveys the history, traditional culture, and contemporary condition of the nations that make up the Haudenosaunee (Iroquois) Confederacy: Seneca, Cayuga, Onondaga, Oneida, Mohawk, and Tuscarora (who were adopted about 1725). We begin before Europeans knew North America.

Like many of the Earth's peoples, the Haudenosaunee, or "People of the Longhouse," whom the French would call the Iroquois and the British would call the Five (later Six) Nations, share a traditional origin story, with North America (which they called "Turtle Island") taking shape on the back of a giant tortoise. Oral history tells us that the nations that would become the Haudenosaunee Confederacy migrated to present-day New York State from southwestward several thousand years ago. Exactly when is not known. They adapted agriculture and domesticated the "three sisters" (corn, squashes, and beans), as they formed a number of largely autonomous groups. The people also evolved a complex ceremonial culture based on the "original instructions" of creation, outlining their relationship with the Earth, its denizens, and each other.

LAND AREA OF THE HAUDENOSAUNEE IN NEW YORK STATE

The aboriginal homeland of the Haudenosaunee stretched from Lake Champlain and the Hudson River in the east, to the Niagara River and Lake Erie in the west, the Delaware River and the central Pennsylvania mountains in the south, and the St. Lawrence River in the north. Included in this region are not only large sections of New York, but also parts of Pennsylvania and Ohio, and Ontario and Québec in Canada. Within this area dwelt many tens of thousands of Iroquois along with refugees from dozens of other nations.

Pequot, Nanticoke, French, English, Africans, Conestoga, Lenni Lenape, Huron, Abenaki, Tutelo, and many others built their communities within Haudenosaunee territory or immigrated to the confederacy as families or individuals.

Within the borders of present-day New York State, the confederacy held active jurisdiction to 80 percent of the state's current area or more than 39,000 of its 49,576 square miles (more than 101,000 of its 128,401 square kilometers). As defined by the Haudenosaunee, each member nation was given custodial responsibility over specific territories. Within this region, the nations were to provide food, shelter, clothing, and medicine for their citizens and visitors while living in a state of ecological balance with other species of life.

THE TRADITIONAL LONGHOUSE

The Haudenosaunee likened their territory to a traditional Longhouse. Samuel de Champlain, one of the first Europeans to

Northeast Woodland Peoples

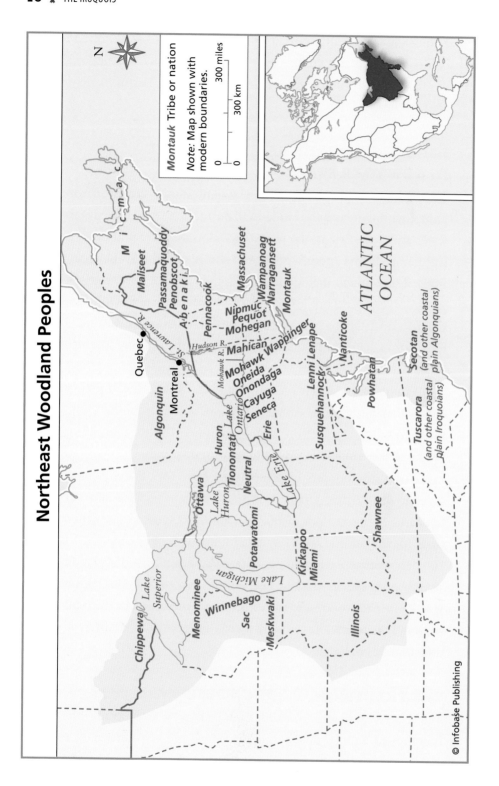

N

Montauk Tribe or nation

Note: Map shown with modern boundaries.

0   300 miles
0   300 km

ATLANTIC OCEAN

Micmac
Maliseet
Passamaquoddy
Penobscot
Abenaki
Pennacook
Massachuset
Nipmuc
Pequot
Mohegan
Wampanoag
Narragansett
Montauk
Mahican
Mohawk Wappinger
Oneida
Onondaga
Cayuga
Seneca
Lenni Lenape
Nanticoke
Susquehannock
Powhatan
Secotan (and other coastal plain Algonquians)
Tuscarora (and other coastal plain Iroquoians)
Erie
St. Lawrence R.
Hudson R.
Mohawk R.
Quebec
Montreal
Algonquin
Huron
Lake Ontario
Tionontati
Neutral
Ottawa
Lake Huron
Potawatomi
Kickapoo
Miami
Shawnee
Lake Erie
Illinois
Lake Michigan
Meskwaki
Sac
Winnebago
Menominee
Chippewa
Lake Superior

© Infobase Publishing

encounter them, described the Haudenosaunee Longhouse in G. Elmore Reaman's *Trail of the Iroquois Indians* (1967) as:

> [A] kind of arbor or bower covered with bark approximately fifty or sixty yards long by twelve wide with a passage ten or twelve feet broad down the middle from one end to the other. Along each side runs a bench four feet above the ground where the inmates [sic] sleep in summer to avoid the innumerable fleas. In winter, they sleep closer to the fire on mats underneath the benches where it is warmer; and they fill the hut with a supply of dry wood to burn at that season. A space is left at one end of the cabin for storing their maize [corn], which they place in large barrels in the middle of the floor; boards suspended overhead preserve their clothing, food, and other things from numerous mice.

Food was stored, according to Lewis Henry Morgan, in *League of the Haudenosaunee, or Iroquois* (1851), "upon cross-poles, near the roof, [where corn was] braided together by the husks. . . . Charred and dried corn and beans were generally stored in bark barrels, and laid away in corners." Surplus corn also was stored underground, in caches (storage bins). Because it was charred and then dried in the sun, the stored corn was nearly immune to diseases of rot brought on by excess moisture. When the corn was exhumed for travel, it was only half as heavy as it had been when fresh.

The Mohawk lived at the eastern entrance of the symbolic Longhouse and were called "Keepers of the Eastern Door." They are also known as the "People of the Flint." Indigenous Mohawk land reached north to the St. Lawrence River (including the Isle of

(Opposite map) Before the Europeans reached North America, Native Americans in the Northeast lived in an area that stretched from Illinois to Maine, and even parts of southern Canada. The members of the Haudenosaunee, or Iroquois, nation lived mostly in New York state.

The longhouse, the traditional Iroquois living structure, typically housed several families and provided storage for food and protection from the weather. Because so many member nations lived in close proximity to each other like a family, the Iroquois liked to compare their territory to a longhouse.

Mont Royal, now the city of Montréal) and south to the Delaware River. Its boundaries included parts of the Adirondack Mountains on the west, Lake Champlain on the east, and the Hudson River north of Albany on the southeast.

Immediately west of the Mohawk Nation lived the Oneida. Their principal communities were clustered southeast of Oneida Lake. The Oneida are known as the "younger brothers" of the Mohawk. They are also called the "People of the Standing Stone." Their homeland extended north-south from the St. Lawrence

River to the Susquehanna River and east-west from Mohawk territory to the middle of Lake Oneida and the Chittenango Creek.

Adjacent to the Oneida, to the west, lived the "People of the Hills," the Onondaga. Their natural borders were Oneida Lake-Chittenango Creek in the east, Lake Ontario-St. Lawrence River to the north, the Susquehanna River to the south, and Skaneateles Lake to the west.

Along the great wetlands of what is now the Montezuma National Wildlife Refuge lived the "People of the Pipe," the Cayuga Nation. Their homelands contained some of the most fertile land in all the Haudenosaunee territory, from Skaneateles Lake west to Seneca Lake and from Lake Ontario south to Pennsylvania. The "People of the Great Hill," commonly known as the Seneca Nation, occupied territory from Seneca Lake to the Niagara River and from Lake Ontario to the Pennsylvania border and far beyond.

The Tuscarora Nation, also called "The Shirt Wearers," returned to Iroquois territory during the first decade of the eighteenth century, about 1725. They established villages on Oneida-Mohawk land along the Susquehanna and Delaware rivers and south of Oneida Lake.

CORN AND THE HAUDENOSAUNEE

Among all the nations of the Haudenosaunee, corn became a staple crop as large-scale political organization developed shortly after A.D. 1000. The Haudenosaunee's ability to produce a surplus of corn was central to the political influence of the confederacy, which reached, through a chain of alliances, from their homelands in present-day upstate New York across much of New England and the Middle Atlantic region.

The Iroquois' implementation of corn-based agriculture, along with the cultivation of beans and squash, played an important role in their adoption of a matrilineal social structure (descent through the female line) and a consensus-based political system. Reliance on corn encouraged agriculture, which was undertaken by the women, to balance the hunting economy, carried on by men. Before roughly A.D. 1000, the Iroquois were less prone to alliance and more frequently disposed to murder for revenge. An older confederacy to the north, possibly the Wyandot (Huron), are said to have sent an emissary, The Peacemaker (Deganawidah), to persuade the Haudenosaunee to make peace with each other and outlaw the blood feud, which was threatening social stability. The Peacemaker and Hiawatha, the Mohawk cofounder of the Haudenosaunee Confederacy, spent most of their adult lives persuading the feuding Haudenosaunee to accept their vision of peace. According to calculations by Barbara A. Mann and Jerry Fields of Toledo University in Ohio, the confederacy was finally accepted in 1142, within living memory, perhaps, of the adoption of corn as a staple crop.

The size of cornfields cultivated by the Haudenosaunee and their neighbors often surprised European-Americans. The Frenchman Marquis de Denonville, who attempted a military conquest of the Haudenosaunee in 1687 (and failed), reported that his forces destroyed more than 400,000 minots of corn. A French minot, according to Lewis Henry Morgan, equals roughly three bushels, so the 400,000 minots of corn that Denonville's forces destroyed was roughly 1.2 million bushels. While Denonville's estimate may have been inflated to please his superiors, even half that amount would have been a very large cache of corn. French troops also found and destroyed a granary that they estimated could hold at least 3 million bushels of corn at the Seneca town of Ganondagan. This estimate (even subject to some statistical inflation) indicated that this site could have been a major source of winter sustenance for the entire Haudenosaunee Confederacy.

The Iroquois also understood the principles of corn breeding. Many of today's hybrid varieties of corn stem from genetic types used long ago by the Iroquois and other Native Americans. Corn was usually planted with squash and beans on small hills. This method of planting promoted high yields because the beans fix nitrogen in their roots that fertilizes the corn and squash. Planting on hills also minimized soil erosion and leaching of nutrients.

Lacrosse was developed as a religious ritual to help heal and honor the sick or dying. Played with wooden sticks and a rubber ball, the game was an important aspect of Iroquois life. Matches involving hundreds of players, with goals set a mile or so apart, could last several days.

Corn and other crops also played a central role in Iroquois ceremonial life, as did sports, especially lacrosse.

SPORTS AND CEREMONY

The Haudenosaunee people often call lacrosse "The Creator's Game." According to Robert W. Venables, writing in *Northeast Indian Quarterly* (Fall, 1989), "Lacrosse is more than a game. It includes religious meanings, purpose, and even ceremony." The playing of lacrosse is said to promote life. A sick person may have a game organized in his or her honor, in the belief that the person's health may improve "simply by seeing that the whole community cared enough to turn out for a game in the sick person's honor." Some traditional lacrosse games are played with a ball laced with herbs and other medicines to help a specific person who is ill.

European explorers, many of them French, observed the Iroquois and other Native Americans playing lacrosse in the seventeenth century. The Jesuits called the game "le jeu de la crosse," because the game stick resembled a bishop's *crosier*, a ceremonial staff.

Before Europeans started to play the game in the mid-nineteenth century, lacrosse matches sometimes involved hundreds of participants playing for several days at a time. Goals could be several miles apart in different villages. When white Canadians started to play the game, rules were regularized and sanctions invoked against payment of players. In 1867, a Mohawk lacrosse team toured England and France, spurring establishment of lacrosse teams there.

The object of the game is to catch a five-ounce (142-gram) hard-rubber ball in a webbed stick and carry it to a goal with the assistance of teammates. Today, lacrosse is played on an area a little larger than a football field. A smaller version, "box lacrosse," is played indoors on a field the size of an ice-hockey rink. Teams usually play 10 to a side in "a spectacular, thundering game of flowing patterns [which] requires great stamina and a head for tactics and technicalities," according to *New York Times* writer Robert Lipsyte.

The spiritual aspects of lacrosse are taught to Iroquois at a young age. The ball used in lacrosse has also been said to represent the moon, which is believed to have formed long ago when a lacrosse ball was thrown into the sky. The game of lacrosse also functioned, during historic times, to keep warriors in physical shape and to sharpen their skills at teamwork between battles. One Iroquois name for the game is *Tewaarathon*, meaning "Little Brother of War."

Lacrosse players are expected to be role models in their communities, and traditional chiefs may remove them from a team if they misbehave. Before the 1994 World Lacrosse Championships in Manchester, England, for example, two players on the Iroquois Nationals were barred from the team after they shoved a Tuscarora woman in a dispute over reservation gambling.

CEREMONY AS A HAUDENOSAUNEE WAY OF LIFE

For the Haudenosaunee, ceremony is a way of life that helps them exist in harmony with the natural world. The Haudenosaunee perform many songs and dances in the Singing Society, the Corn Husk Society, and the False Face Society, among others, which preserve traditional knowledge. The Creator provided the Haudenosaunee three major songs and dances: The Great Feather Dance, the Drum Dance, and the Atonwa or Personal Chant. The Great Feather Dance honors the Creator and the good mind of the people. The Drum Dance song shows respect and appreciation to all the things the Creator has provided the *Onkwehshon:a* (the people) during their daily lives. The Atonwa is sung to begin a ceremony at which children are named, to connect an infant with the natural world.

The Haudenosaunee open and close important events with their Thanksgiving Address, the *Ohen:ton Karihwatehkwen*, which translates to "Words Before All Else." The Thanksgiving Address brings all minds together as one and expresses appreciation to all life on Earth and elsewhere in the universe for following the Creator's original instructions. Mother Earth is thanked, along with the plants (with special notice to the medicine plants and the trees). The thunderers, the waters, the birds, and the four-legged and two-legged animals are also thanked, along with the four winds, the fish, the stars, the sun, Grandmother Moon, the teachers, and the Creator. All are thanked for following the Creator's original instructions on how they should live, for by following the original instructions, the Great Circle of Life is continued in balance.

The Haudenosaunee honor nature in a yearlong ceremonial cycle that follows the growing season. The six-day Midwinter Ceremony (*Tsiothohrko:wa*, which translates to "the Big Cold"), in January, signals a new solar cycle. Day one of Midwinter includes the stirring of the ashes, which represents the joining of community. Day two features the Great Feather Dance, which is performed for the Creator and acknowledges the one mind of the people. On other days, the ceremony includes the singing of the

Atonwa, a performance of the Drum Dance, and the playing of the Peach Bowl Game, which helps people remember that what they have around them is not theirs.

The Sap Ceremony, in February, is called *Enniska* (Lateness); in March it is called *Ennisko:wa* (Much Lateness). The Thunder Dance and Maple Ceremony are held in March and April, which is *Onerahtokha* (Budding Time). The Thunder Dance, held as spring comes, honors water life. The Seed Ceremony, *Onerahtokhako:wa* (Time of the Big Leaf), is held in May to honor the seeds that will germinate and feed the people. The Moon Ceremony is held in early June, *Ohiariha* (Ripening Time), and in early fall during October. The Moon Ceremony honors Grandmother Moon, women, and all female life that perpetuates the Great Circle of Life. The Strawberry Ceremony, held in June, honors the medicine plants and other plants with healing powers. The Bean Ceremony, *Ohiarihko:wa* (Time of Much Ripening), is held in July, and August, as *Seskeha* (Time of Freshness). The Green Corn Ceremony also is held in August.

The Harvest Ceremony, in October, expresses gratitude for the good fortune of the growing season. Another Thunder Ceremony is held in November and called *Kentenko:wa* (Time of Much Poverty)—again, as in the spring, to honor water life. The last ceremony of the calendar year is the End of Season Ceremony, in December, *Tsiothohrha* (Time of Cold), which expresses thankfulness for the year that has passed, with preparations for the coming year.

Iroquois ceremonial culture took place within a political context, as several nations joined in a confederacy to stem revenge killings. The Iroquois League of Peace would influence North American history for centuries to come.

The Iroquois
Form a National
Government

I roquois law and customs have filtered into general North American society. For example, the idea of "sleeping on it" comes directly from the debating practices of the Iroquois Grand Council, which made no important decision the same day a proposal was introduced, to allow tempers to cool. The Iroquois' political structure also provided a model for a federal system being developed by the founders of the United States. To "bury the hatchet" is also an Iroquois idiom, a reference to the founding of the confederacy, as the member nations threw their weapons of war into a large pit under the Great Tree of Peace.

Many of these Haudenosaunee contributions to general culture in the United States first took place during a long period of trade, diplomacy, and occasional war (roughly 1600 to 1800). The Haudenosaunee were important players in the contest for North America that was being waged by European powers, principally

Britain and France. The Haudenosaunee were a focal point for diplomacy by the French and the British, which allowed some of those who would be influential in founding the United States (most notably Benjamin Franklin) to observe the Haudenosaunee political system firsthand.

The Haudenosaunee's Great Law of Peace (*Kaianerekowa*) has been passed from generation to generation by use of wampum, a form of written communication that outlines a complex system of checks and balances between clans, nations, and genders. A complete oral recitation of the Great Law can take several days; several versions of it have been translated into English and provide one reason the Iroquois have been cited so often in debates regarding the origins of United States fundamental law. While many other Native confederacies existed along the borders of the British colonies, most of the specific provisions of their governments have been lost.

HOW OLD IS THE IROQUOIS CONFEDERACY?

The Haudenosaunee Confederacy, one of the world's oldest democracies, is at least three centuries older than most previous estimates, according to research by Barbara A. Mann and Jerry Fields of Toledo University in Ohio. They believe that the confederacy was founded almost 1,000 years ago. The date that Mann and Fields assert for the founding of the Iroquois Confederacy is more than 300 years earlier than the previous consensus of scholarship; many experts had dated the formation of the confederacy to 1451, at the time of a solar eclipse. Seneca oral history mentions that they adopted the Great Law of Peace shortly after a "sign in the sky," believed to be a total eclipse of the sun. Mann and Fields contend that the 1451 eclipse was total, but that its shadow fell over Pennsylvania, well to the southwest of the ratifying council's location.

Using a combination of documentary sources, solar-eclipse data, and Iroquois oral history, Mann and Fields contend that the

Hoping to establish peace, the Peacemaker Deganawidah and Hiawatha, a Mohawk leader, set out to convince other Haudenosaunee chiefs to accept the Great Law. Their biggest opposition was Tadadaho, a chief who was said to be so horrifying he had snakes for hair and a twisted body.

confederacy's body of law was adopted by the Seneca (the last of the five nations to ratify it) at the end of August 1142. The ratification council convened at a site that is now a high-school football field in Victor, New York. Mann estimated that the journey of the Peacemaker (Deganawidah) and Hiawatha in support of the Great Law began about a quarter-century earlier with the Mohawk, at the Eastern Door of the confederacy.

The struggle to form a unifying law by the formerly strife-torn Iroquois nations was, by all measures, an epic account full of stories that defy ordinary reality. No doubt, as with many founding myths, actual events have been embellished over time. The Peacemaker, for example, sometimes traveled in a stone canoe. The evil Onondaga wizard Tadadaho, the main opponent of the new law, was so overpoweringly ugly that he had snakes for hair. After a long battle, Tadadaho came to accept the Great Law of Peace. His name became the title of the confederacy's chief executive.

This indigenous American epic has been compared to the Greeks' *Iliad* and *Odyssey*, the Mayans' Popol Vuh, and the

The Iroquois and Gender Equity

Some sections of the Great Law of Peace gave the gantowisas (women acting in their official capacities) ownership of the land, along with the power to keep and bestow lineage names; adopt or expel citizens; nominate officials to positions as chiefs, clan mothers, or warriors; impeach errant officials; and approve or deny the male leaders' plans for wars. The men's sections concerned relations with outside nations, federal councils, warfare, and national treason. Thus, while nearly all of the people who were prominent in Iroquois historical narrative were male, they held their positions at the consent of women.

According to Mann, writing in *The Encyclopedia of the Haudenosaunee (Iroquois Confederacy)*, published in 2000, "It is wildly erroneous to focus on the operations of the men's councils while ignoring the operations of the women's councils. Unfortunately, this is the approach of nearly every western treatment of League government, leaving the mistaken impression that women were secondary or subservient to men. In fact, some western anthropologists, including Elisabeth Tooker, and ethnologists, including Lewis Henry Morgan, have actually gone so far as to state that this was the case." *Jigonsaseh* was the position title of the Head Clan Mother of the Haudenosaunee League. Her many titles include: "The Mother of Nations," "The Peace Queen," "The Great Woman," "The Fire Woman," and "The Maize Maiden."

Tibetan Book of the Dead. The most complete written version of the founding epic runs to 800 pages (half in Onondaga, half in English); to recite it orally took the Cayuga Jacob Thomas, the last person capable of such a recitation in Onondaga (during the 1990s), four eight-hour days.

The Jigonsaseh's traditional obligations included feeding all visitors, such as war parties, regardless of their national loyalties, and discovering what their business was in Iroquoia. All visitors were safe within the precincts of *Gaustauyea*, her hometown; her Longhouse was a place of absolute sanctuary. Jigonsaseh was charged with making and keeping the peace among individuals, clans, and nations, using mediation and negotiation. In circumstances when the use of force became unavoidable, she had the right to raise and command armies. She also convened all the meetings of the Clan Mothers' Councils, to discuss the business of the people and to forward the Mothers' consensus agenda to the men's Grand Council, sitting at Onondaga. The civil chiefs could not consider any matter that had not been sent forward by the Jigonsaseh on behalf of the gantowisas.

While a high degree of gender equity existed in Iroquois law, gender roles often were (and remain today) very carefully defined, right down to the version of history passed down by people of either gender. The vast majority of anthropological informants who were male tended to play up the role of Deganawidah and Hiawatha, which was written into history. Women who would have described the role of Jigonsaseh were usually not consulted. "Jigonsaseh is recalled by the Keepers as a cofounder of the League, alongside of Deganawidah and Hiawatha," Mann writes. "Her name has been obliterated from the white record because her story was a woman's story and nineteenth-century male ethnographers simply failed to ask women, whose story hers was, about the history of the League."

THE GREAT WHITE PINE

In his vision that united the Haudenosaunee, the Peacemaker saw a giant white pine reaching to the sky, gaining strength from counterbalancing principles of life. The first rule was that a stable mind and a healthy body should be in balance, aiding peace between individuals and groups. Second, the Peacemaker stated that humane conduct, thought, and speech were necessary for equity and justice among peoples.

The Great White Pine serves throughout the Great Law as a metaphor for the confederacy. Its branches shelter the people of the nations, and its roots spread in all directions, inviting other peoples, regardless of race or nationality, to take shelter under the tree. The Haudenosaunee recognize no bars to dual citizenship; in fact, many influential figures in the English colonies and early United States were adopted into Iroquois nations.

On top of the symbolic white pine, an eagle is perched. The Peacemaker explained that the tree is humanity, living within the principles governing relations among human beings. The eagle (a symbol also adopted by the United States) is humanity's lookout against enemies who would disturb the peace.

THE IROQUOIS' FEDERAL GOVERNMENT

The Peacemaker's vision established a federal government that united the Haudenosaunee nations. The central Grand Council at Onondaga seats 50 chiefs (one seat is kept empty for the Peacemaker, who is said to be present in spirit). Each position on the council represents a matrilineal lineage (*owachira*). A chief for each lineage is "raised up" by consensus of the clan mothers holding the rights to that lineage, who are charged with polling the opinions of the people whom the chief will represent. The same clan mothers may impeach a sitting chief for any of a wide range of misbehaviors that undermine confidence in him, from missing too many meetings to murder. A peace chief may never use violence. Chiefs enjoy great prestige but have very little coercive power.

The white pine tree would become a symbol of the league, as its boughs stretch out and protect member nations while its roots reach out and invite others to join and participate in peace. Atop the tree is an eagle, a lookout against enemies who threaten the peace, and buried underneath is a war club.

According to *A Basic Call to Consciousness*, published by Mohawks at Akwesasne, "Peace was to be defined not as the simple absence of war or strife, but as the active striving of humans for the purpose of establishing universal justice. Peace was defined as the product of a society which strives to establish concepts which correlate with the English words *power*, *reason*, and *righteousness*."

Each of the six nations maintains its own council, whose sachems (or chiefs) are also nominated by the clan mothers of families holding hereditary rights to office titles. The Grand Council is drawn from the individual national councils. The Grand Council may also nominate sachems outside the hereditary structure, based on merit alone. These sachems, called "pine tree chiefs," were said to have sprung from the body of the people as the symbolic Great White Pine springs from the Earth.

The Great Law also included provisions guaranteeing freedom of religion and the right of redress (an individual's request to solve a problem) before the Grand Council. It also forbade unauthorized entry of homes—all measures that sound familiar to United States citizens through the Bill of Rights. If the Council will not act on the will of the people, sachems face removal under other provisions. Through public opinion and debate, the Great Law gave the Iroquois people basic rights within a distinctive and representative governmental framework.

The League of the Iroquois has long been a family-oriented government that has a constitution with a fixed corpus of laws concerned with mutual defense. Through the elimination of blood feuds between clans, the state is granted a monopoly on legally sanctioned violence. This process brings peace through a fundamental social contract. Unity, peace, and brotherhood are balanced against the natural rights of all people and the necessity to share resources equitably. Unity for mutual defense is an abiding concept within the league. The Iroquois imagery of unity is a bundle of five or six arrows tied together to symbolize the complete union of the nations and the unbroken strength that such a unity portrays.

The Iroquois also have built-in checks and balances through consensus based on public opinion. The notion of federalism pervades the entire structure. The central council handles external matters such as war, peace, and treaty making. The Grand Council cannot interfere with the internal affairs of the individual nations. Each nation has its own sachems, but they are limited in that they may deal only with their nation's relations with others in the confederacy.

The Iroquois, having built alliances across a wide area, would soon meet European explorers, followed by traders and immigrants, in an encounter that would spill blood and shape ideas in ways that would impact both the Native Americans and the immigrants.

Early Iroquois Contacts with Europeans

Jacques Cartier, a French navigator, set sail from France on April 20, 1534, with a crew of 61 men in two ships. After crossing the Atlantic Ocean, he sailed up the St. Lawrence River, seeking the Northwest Passage, and hit the Iroquois Confederacy instead. He encountered an Iroquoian group he called "the Laurentians" living on Anticosti Island, at the outlet of the St. Lawrence River.

Meanwhile, on July 24 at the Bay of Gaspé, Cartier claimed North America for France by erecting a 30-foot (9-meter) cross emblazoned with *fleurs-de-lys* and the words *Vive le Roi de France* ("Long live the king of France") over objections from resident Iroquois. According to Mohawk tradition, cited by Barbara A. Mann, the Iroquois seemed to realize that a foreign sovereign was claiming their land. They recited the roll call of the chiefs of the Haudenosaunee League to prove their prior claim to the land. Cartier himself recorded in his papers that their orator and primary chief, Donnacona, "pointed to the land . . . as if he wished to say that all this region belonged to him, and that we ought not to have set up this cross without his permission." Cartier dismissed these passionate objections as a "harangue."

Cartier was seeking gold and a Northwest Passage through North America to India and China, but he found neither. (He thought that the St. Lawrence River might take him to Asia.) Instead, he kidnapped two Iroquoians at Gaspé—Dom Agaya and Taignoagny, sons of Chief Donnacona. He then sailed back to France to show them as proof that he had reached North America. Cartier arrived home at Saint-Malo in northwestern France on September 5, 1534. The sight of the Iroquois stirred great interest at the French court, where various courtiers thought that Dom Agaya and Taignoagny were Aztecs, Mayas, or Incas kidnapped by the Spanish. Like the Spanish, the French assumed that human habitation indicated access to wealth awaiting French exploitation.

Cartier did not deny these assumptions as he solicited funds for a second voyage. He set sail for America on May 19, 1535, with Dom Agaya and Taignoagny. The two Iroquois had learned French while in captivity, and so they led Cartier up the St. Lawrence River into Stadacona (present-day Québec), at the harbor of Sainte-Croix. Having long realized that Cartier was seeking gold, silver, spices, and copper, Dom Agaya and Taignoagny tried to divert Cartier away from Iroquoia with tales of a mysterious "Kingdom of Saguenay," which they said contained what he wanted, as well as a population of friendly Europeans.

Cartier made landfall at Stadacona, Dom Agaya and Taignoagny's home (near modern-day Québec City). Friends of the men embraced them and refused Cartier's demands that they return to his custody. They had some leverage: Cartier needed guides to find Hochelaga, a large Iroquoian city at the foot of the Lachine Rapids at modern-day Montréal. Cartier left most of his 119-man crew at Stadacona and, with Native guides, a niece and

The Iroquois did not welcome the arrival of Jacques Cartier, and they did not appreciate the cross, a symbol of France's claim over the New World, that he erected on the beach. Cartier ignored their protests. When he did not get what he wanted from the Iroquois, he took some of them hostage in order to gain leverage. Above, Cartier looks on as his men battle the Iroquois.

a son of Donnacona's, and a few fellow Frenchmen, traveled to Hochelaga, imagining that a Northwest Passage lay just upriver. Encountering steep rapids, he was forced to stay in Stadacona for the winter before voyaging back to France, empty-handed. In order to convince the French of the Kingdom of Saguenay's existence, Cartier kidnapped Chief Donnacona, his sons, and a handful of children he had been given as gifts.

Cartier tried a third time, in 1541. King Francis I planned to forestall the Spanish with a colony on the St. Lawrence. He therefore dispatched a colonization team headed by a French nobleman, Jean-François de La Rocque de Roberval, who was to direct the activities of Cartier. The fact that Francis I promoted Roberval over Cartier suggested that the king no longer believed Cartier's stories. Cartier, finding nothing of value to Europeans, took more prisoners.

By 1541, nine of Cartier's ten prisoners, including Donnacona, Dom Agaya, and Taignoagny, had died in French captivity, having been baptized by Catholic priests. Cartier found some quartz and (probably) pyrite that he convinced himself were diamonds and gold. He departed for France the following spring, only, according to Mann, writing in *The Encyclopedia of the Haudenosaunee*, "to be intercepted at Newfoundland by Roberval (who was only just arriving, a whole year late). Roberval, an aristocrat who knew gold and diamonds when he saw them, angrily ordered Cartier back to his Canadian post but, perhaps knowing the welcome that awaited him there, Cartier decided to chance fate by absconding in the middle of the night, sneaking back to France with his prize."

Once in France, Cartier's prize was immediately revealed to be worthless, and he never received another commission from the crown. For his part, Roberval was summarily kicked out of "New France" by the thoroughly disgusted Iroquois who, having had their fill of bad-mannered visitors, refused to allow him to establish a colony on their lands.

SAMUEL DE CHAMPLAIN EXPLORES FOR FRANCE

Samuel de Champlain, another French explorer, came into contact with the Haudenosaunee in 1609, more than half a century after Cartier's voyages. Champlain did not understand that the Iroquois maintained alliances with other Native American peoples in much of northeastern North America or that their territories stood along the best trade route between the East Coast of North America and the continent's interior, a matter of vital importance at a time when most trade (not to mention military forces) traveled by water. If Champlain had known how important the Haudenosaunee would become to the future of the French and British rivalry in North America, he might have watched his diplomatic manners. Instead, he quickly engaged a band of Mohawk in armed conflict and killed several of them near the north shore of the lake that now bears his name.

This was another chapter in a generally sour relationship between the French and the Haudenosaunee that continued until the French were expelled from North America at the end of the French and Indian (also known as the Seven Years) War in 1763. Champlain's behavior was still being cited during the 1750s when the Iroquois created an alliance with the British, hastening the French decline as a world colonial power. Despite popular myths that Champlain knew how to respect and get along with Native Americans, evidence indicates that he refused wampum payments to compensate for the murders of Frenchmen by Indians, creating tension.

Champlain was an associate of Pierre Du Gua, sieur de Monts, who was granted by the French government the right to assign tracts of land in North America, as well as a 10-year monopoly on the fur trade. In 1608, Champlain's small expeditionary force built a fort on the site of present-day Québec City, intending to participate in the fur trade. Twenty of twenty-eight Frenchmen on the colonizing expedition died during the first winter from disease, harsh weather, and military altercations with American Indians. By 1620, only 60 people lived in the fort. Even by 1650, 15 years

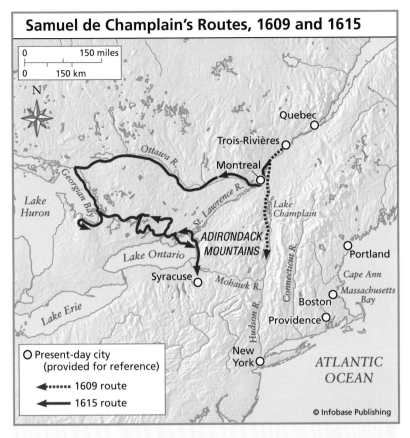

Samuel de Champlain's Routes, 1609 and 1615

0 — 150 miles
0 — 150 km

N

Quebec

Trois-Rivières

Ottawa R.

Montreal

Georgian Bay

St. Lawrence R.

Lake Huron

Lake Champlain

ADIRONDACK MOUNTAINS

Lake Ontario

Syracuse

Mohawk R.

Connecticut R.

Portland

Cape Ann

Massachusetts Bay

Boston

Lake Erie

Hudson R.

Providence

O Present-day city (provided for reference)

◄······ 1609 route

◄——— 1615 route

New York

ATLANTIC OCEAN

© Infobase Publishing

When Samuel de Champlain came to North America, he exacerbated already tense relations between the Iroquois and France. Although Champlain explored much of the region around Quebec and established the first successful North American settlement, he struggled without the help of the Iroquois.

after Champlain died, New France amounted to only about 2,000 people in a chain of isolated villages that stretched for almost 750 miles (1,200 kilometers) along the St. Lawrence River.

THE "BEAVER WARS"

The name "Beaver Wars" has become historical shorthand for the Haudenosaunee campaign against the Wyandot (Huron), which culminated in their defeat and assimilation by the Haudenosaunee about 1650. Like most wars, this one had more than one initiating cause. The most prominent reason for the antipathy leading to the war, however, was competition over diminishing stocks of beaver and other fur-bearing animals. The Haudenosaunee cause during this conflict was aided immeasurably by their relatively recent acquisition of European firearms, which the Wyandot, for the most part, lacked. The Mohawk, situated near trading centers at Albany and Montréal, were among the first to acquire a stock of firearms; one French source estimated that they had close to 300 guns by 1643.

At the beginning of the seventeenth century, the Wyandot, who lived near Georgian Bay on Lake Huron, were a prosperous confederacy of 25,000 to 30,000 people, comparable to their adversaries, the Haudenosaunee. By 1642, the Wyandot had allied solidly with the French and had also entered an alliance with the Susquehannok, south of the Iroquois, who felt as if a military vise was being closed around them. In 1642, 1645, and 1647, the Haudenosaunee tried to secure peace with the French, to no avail. After the third try, they decided to break the alliance. The Wyandot had built a confederacy similar in structure to the Haudenosaunee (although more geographically compact).

By 1640, the Wyandot economy was nearly totally dependent on trade with the French. At the same time, as they were weakened by disease, the Wyandot found themelves facing waves of raids by the Iroquois (principally Mohawk and Seneca), who were seeking to capture the Wyandot's share of the fur trade. The Mohawk had been exposed to European trade goods earlier than the Wyandot and may have been looking for more furs to finance trade. The Wyandot's location at the center of several trade routes also made them an appealing point of attack at a time when demand was rising for beaver pelts and the available supply of the animals was declining.

For nearly a decade, the Mohawk and Seneca harassed the Wyandot. The Wyandot, fearing Iroquois attacks, sometimes curtailed their trade with the French during the 1640s. Between 1647

(continues on page 42)

The Iroquois and the Fur Trade

Across much of North America, Native Americans initially became part of the European cash economy through the fur trade. The type of animal harvested varied (from beaver in the Northeast to deer in the southeast, bear in the Rocky Mountains, and sea otters along the Alaskan coast, for example), but the economic system was largely the same. The fur trade flourished in most areas until the early to mid-nineteenth century, after which it was curtailed by the near-extinction of some species, as well as changes in European fashions, especially coats and headgear.

Native American men harvested most of the furs, while Native women prepared the skins for market. Native people also provided many goods and services that supported the fur trade, such as corn, maple sugar, wild rice, canoes, and snowshoes. The fur trade brought social as well as economic change to Native American societies. The number of men with more than one wife increased in some Plains cultures because an individual male hunter could employ more than one woman tanner.

The Iroquois were important in the regional fur trade, as well as in diplomacy and war. In exchange for furs, the Iroquois received trade goods such as iron needles and knives, as well as prized copper kettles. European traders soon learned to sell the Indians kettles made of thinner metal, because they cost less to manufacture and wore out more quickly, increasing sales.

Epidemics, first of measles, then of smallpox, reached Haudenosaunee country with the fur trade, peaking in 1634 and 1635. Societies and economies were severely stressed. The Mohawk population dropped from 7,740 to 2,830 within a matter of months. Firearms reached the Haudenosaunee

(continues)

(continued)

within a generation of the fur trade. In 1639, the Dutch tried, without success, to outlaw the sale of guns to Indians. By 1648, Dutch merchants in Albany were enthusiastic participants in the firearms trade, in part because the use of guns increased Native Americans' productivity as harvesters of beaver and other fur-bearing animals.

The fur trade eroded Indians' inhibitions against the killing of animals above and beyond their own needs. In New England, beaver populations ceased to be commercially exploitable after 1660, but animals continued to be harvested in areas that had been reached in later years. By the nineteenth century, however, beaver had been hunted to below sustainable levels in most of North America, and European hat styles had changed, sparing the few surviving beavers in North America.

(continued from page 40)

and 1650, a final Iroquois drive swept over the Wyandot homeland, provoking the dissolution of their confederacy, as well as the seizure of the Wyandot fur-trading business by the Seneca and Mohawk.

Iroquois pressure against the Wyandot continued for several years after the conclusion of the Beaver Wars, as Wyandot refugees sought new homes throughout the Great Lakes and St. Lawrence Valley. Many refugees experienced acute hunger, and a sizable number starved during this diaspora. Some Wyandot became so hungry that they ate human excrement; others dug up the bodies of the dead and ate them. This was done in desperation, and with great shame, because cannibalism is directly contrary to Wyandot belief and custom.

Scattered communities of Wyandot gradually revived traditional economies after the hungry years of the 1650s. Many Wyandot settled in or near European communities (including Jesuit missions). Even those who became Christianized and Europeanized continued to live in Longhouses during these years.

They continued to hunt and trap as much as possible, and to practice slash-and-burn agriculture.

True to their own traditions, the Haudenosaunee adopted a number of Wyandot refugees after the Beaver Wars and socialized them into various Iroquois families and clans. The Iroquois were replenishing their societies, which had been hard hit by European diseases and the casualties of continual war.

THE BRITISH AND THE IROQUOIS

When the British first met the Iroquois, they adapted to the Iroquois' style of diplomacy, recognizing that the Haudenosaunee's wide web of alliances could be used to spread British influence. The British styled the relationship as a Covenant Chain, a diplomatic metaphor for the alliance. As with many Native American nations during the days of early contact with Europeans, the Haudenosaunee carried out trade and diplomacy in the context of an extended family. In William N. Fenton's words, the Covenant Chain represented a "network of symbolic kinship." When diplomacy was cordial, the chain was being "shined." If the two sides fell into disagreement, the chain was "rusting."

The Covenant Chain was first used as a metaphor for the alliance at a treaty concluded in Albany in 1677. Before that, the most common metaphor for alliance had been a rope. For a brief period while the Dutch were active in trade, the rope became an iron chain, which was converted to an image of a silver chain under the British. For a time, the Massachusetts Bay Colony tried to gain an advantage in trade by calling its chain "golden," but the effort failed.

HENDRICK (TIYANOGA), IROQUOIS LEADER

Later, in the eighteenth century, this alliance played an important role as the British and French battled for colonial domination in North America. The Mohawk leader Hendrick (Tiyanoga) was perhaps the most important individual link in the chain of alliance that saved the New York frontier and probably New England from the French in the initial stages of the Seven Years War, which was called the French and Indian War in North America.

The Covenant Chain was a serious matter to Hendrick. In June 1753, for example, he led 17 Mohawk in demanding an audience with Governor George Clinton in New York City. Hendrick angrily told Clinton that the English were not adequately protecting the Mohawk from the French and that English squatters were taking large areas of Mohawk land. "The Covenant Chain is broken between you and us," Hendrick told Clinton, in Donald A. Grinde Jr. and Bruce E. Johansen's *Exemplar of Liberty*, as the Mohawk stormed out of his office. William Johnson, the English Indian agent to the Iroquois and an adopted Mohawk, later criticized Hendrick for treating Clinton in an uncivil manner. At the same time, Johnson did his best to provide the English protection that Hendrick had sought. One result of his effort was the Albany Congress of 1754, at which Hendrick picked up a stick and threw it behind his back, lecturing the English: "You have thus thrown us behind your back, and disregarded us, whereas the French are a subtle and vigilant people, ever using their utmost endeavors to seduce and bring our people over to them."

Well-known as a man of distinction in his manners and dress, Hendrick visited England again in 1740. At that time, King George II presented him with an ornate green coat of satin, fringed in gold, which Hendrick was fond of wearing in combination with his Mohawk clothing. At Johnson Hall, William Johnson's estate, Tiyanoga had many opportunities to rub elbows with visiting English nobles. Sometimes he arrived in war paint, fresh from battle. Thomas Pownall, a shrewd observer of colonial Indian affairs, described Hendrick in a letter to a colleague as "a bold artful, intriguing Fellow [who] has learnt no small share of European Politics, [and who] obstructs and opposes all [business] where he has not been talked to first . . ."

The Frenchman Hector Saint Jean de Crevecoeur, an adopted Haudenosaunee who participated in sessions of the Grand Council

THE ALBANY CONGRESS · 1754

WHENEVER A PEOPLE
OR AN INSTITUTION
FORGETS ITS HARD BEGINNINGS
IT IS BEGINNING TO DECAY
CARL SANDBURG 1963

The Albany Congress convened in 1754. Delegates from all 13 colonies were in attendance, as well as some Iroquois. Benjamin Franklin proposed and revised the Albany Plan, a proposal that would help preserve the union of the colonies against the French and also keep the peace with the Native Americans. Above, a mural depicts Benjamin Franklin and his son meeting the governors of various states at the Albany Congress.

at Onondaga, described Hendrick in late middle age, in his book *Letters from an American Farmer*. Here, Hendrick prepared for dinner at the Johnson estate, within a few years of the Albany Congress:

> [He] wished to appear at his very best. . . . His head was shaved, with the exception of a little tuft of hair in the back, [to] which he attached a piece of silver. To the cartilage of his ears . . . he attached a little brass wire twisted into very tight spirals. . . . A girondole was hung from his nose. Wearing a wide silver

neckpiece, a crimson vest and a blue cloak adorned with sparkling gold, Hendrick, as was his custom, shunned European breeches for a loincloth fringed with glass beads. On his feet, Hendrick wore moccasins of tanned elk, embroidered with porcupine quills, fringed with tiny silver bells.

In 1754, Hendrick attended the conference at Albany that framed a colonial plan of union. By the time Hendrick was invited to address colonial delegates at the congress, he was well known on both sides of the Atlantic, among Iroquois and Europeans alike. Hendrick had played a major role in convening the Albany Congress in large part because he wished to see his friend Johnson reinstated as the English superintendent of affairs with the Six Nations. Without Johnson's aid, Hendrick maintained that the Covenant Chain would rust. It was Johnson himself who conducted most of the day-to-day business with the Indians at Albany.

A little more than a year after the congress, Hendrick died maintaining the Covenant Chain at the Battle of Lake George on September 8, 1755, as Johnson defeated Baron Dieskau. He was shot from his horse and bayoneted to death while on a scouting party.

FRANKLIN'S ROLE AT THE ALBANY CONGRESS

Benjamin Franklin, also a key figure at the Albany Congress, observed the diplomatic images evoked by the Covenant Chain early in his distinguished career after he attended an Iroquois condolence council at Carlisle, Pennsylvania. At this treaty with the Iroquois and Ohio Indians (Twightee, Delaware, Shawnee, and Wyandot), Franklin watched the Oneida chief, Scarrooyady, and a Mohawk, Cayanguileguoa, condole the Ohio Indians for their losses against the French. Franklin listened while Scarrooyady recounted the origins of the Great Law to the Ohio Indians, as related in *Exemplar of Liberty*:

We must let you know, that there was a friendship established by our and your Grandfathers, and a mutual Council fire was kindled. In this friendship all those then under the ground, who had not yet obtained eyes or faces (that is, those unborn) were included; and it was then mutually promised to tell the same to their children and children's children.

Having condoled the Ohio Indians, Scarrooyady, according to *Exemplar of Liberty*, exhorted all assembled to "preserve this Union and Friendship, which has so long and happy continued among us. Let us keep the chain from rusting." Franklin later used the Covenant Chain image in designs for early United States coins, mixing ideas from both cultures in a manner that was common in this century of revolutions in which the Iroquois played a key role in the continental military contest between Great Britain and France.

The Iroquois Role in a Century of Revolutions

During most of the eighteenth century, the Haudenosaunee were important power brokers in the diplomacy of their region, playing off French and British immigrants. They played a significant role between the British loyalists and the American patriots in the American Revolution. (George Washington's army might have starved at Valley Forge without Oneida corn.) The confederacy split over which side to support. At this time, diplomacy in this area was conducted according to Iroquois rules, with the idea that newcomers were guests on Turtle Island (North America). Treaties were important events, so much so that Benjamin Franklin sold the printed proceedings in small books to an avid audience.

THE LANCASTER TREATY COUNCIL

One of the more momentous treaty councils between the Haudenosaunee, their Native American allies, and delegates of the

Colonial authorities met with delegates from the Iroquois confederacy to hammer out a territorial agreement. Canassatego *(above)*, a political leader of the Iroquois, signed the Treaty of Lancaster, a document that passed ownership of unclaimed lands North and West of Virginia to the U.S. government.

Middle Atlantic colonies, including Pennsylvania and Virginia, took place at Lancaster, Pennsylvania, during the summer of 1744. Lancaster was a frontier settlement at the time, a trading center between British settlements, the Iroquois, and their allies.

According to one unnamed observer, quoted in *The Encyclopedia of the Haudenosaunee*, the Tadadaho (speaker of the confederacy) Canassatego "strode into town . . . [and] ran the show. . . . He dined and drank and joked with the colonial gentlemen, and he collected a quite satisfactory payment for the lands . . . to which the Iroquois claimed a right of conquest." At the same time, the delegates from Virginia got Canassatego's consent for their own version of empire building. Canassatego signed a deed that gave Virginia, at least on paper, settlement rights according to

(continues on page 52)

Sir William Johnson, British Indian Agent

Sir William Johnson's friendship with the Iroquois helped push the French out of North America.

Sir William Johnson was probably the most influential Englishman in relations with the Haudenosaunee and their allies during the French and Indian War (1754–1763). The British and the French were fighting in North America, as an extension of their rivalry in Europe; both were appealing for Iroquois alliance.

From Johnson Hall, his mansion near Albany, Johnson forayed on Indian war parties, painting himself like an Iroquois and taking part in ceremonial dances. He was a close friend of the Mohawk leader whom the English called Hendrick (his native name was Tiyanoga). Johnson often traveled with Tiyanoga as a warrior.

Johnson emigrated to America from Ireland in 1738, establishing a plantation from which he traded with the Haudenosaunee, especially the Mohawk, gaining their trust. At the beginning of the French and Indian War, Johnson was commissioned as British superintendent of Indian Affairs for the northern district, making him the main British liaison with the Haudenosaunee and many of their allies. Johnson kept the post until he died in 1774, steering the Mohawk successfully into an alliance with the British Crown against French interests. This alliance persisted through the American Revolution under the direction of his nephew, Guy Johnson.

Because he successfully recruited a sizable number of Iroquois to the British interest, Johnson was made a baronet,

"Sir William Johnson," with a £5,000 award. From his home, Johnson learned the customs and language of the Mohawk. He had a number of children by Mohawk women and acknowledged them as such. He had several other children by his wife, Mary "Molly" Brant, a Mohawk clan mother and granddaughter of Hendrick. Johnson was well-liked, particularly among the Mohawk. Hendrick had a high regard for the Englishman. One of the main agenda items at the Albany Congress in 1754 was Hendrick's demand that Johnson be maintained as the British Indian agent.

In June 1760, in the final thrust to defeat the French in North America, Johnson called for an attack on Montréal. About 600 warriors responded. Many Native Americans living in the Montréal area also responded to his call. Johnson reported that he was sending gifts to "foreign Indians" who were switching their allegiance from the sinking French Empire. By August 5, 1760, the native contingent had reached 1,330.

The defeat of the French and their departure from Canada at the end of the war in 1763 upset the balance of power that the Haudenosaunee had sought to maintain. They could no longer play one European power against another. The English now occupied all the forts surrounding Iroquois country. Johnson played a key role in pressing the British Crown to limit immigration west of the Appalachians, but land-hungry settlers ignored edicts such as the Royal Proclamation of 1763, which sought to limit land seizures, intensifying conflicts over land. In the meantime, Johnson became one of the richest men in the colonies through his land transactions and trade with the Iroquois and their allies.

During October and November of 1768, Johnson hosted a major treaty with the Haudenosaunee nations, the Delaware, the Seneca of Ohio, the Shawnee, and others at Fort Stanwix, near present-day Rome, New York. Substantial amounts of land were ceded by the Six Nations, acting as agents for all the

(continues)

(continued)

Indians, in negotiations with representatives of New Jersey, Pennsylvania, and Virginia. After the treaty was negotiated, the British Crown told Johnson that he had taken too much land and ordered some of it returned to the Indians. Boundaries were confirmed, and the Covenant Chain brightened.

The aging Sir William, his face pockmarked with signs of advancing syphilis, died on July 11, 1774, during a meeting with the Iroquois at his mansion. For two hours, Johnson addressed the Iroquois in the oratorical style he had learned from them, summoning them to the British cause in the coming American Revolution. Suddenly, Johnson collapsed. He was carried to bed, where he died two hours later. His sudden death stunned the assembly of chiefs.

(continued from page 49)

the colony's charter. The charter had no well-defined western or northern boundary, so Canassatego was, in theory, signing away all of the present-day United States north and west of Virginia (except the lands explicitly claimed by the Haudenosaunee) all the way to the Pacific Ocean. No one at that time realized how far away that ocean was. Canassatego clearly did not understand the scope of the agreement.

HAUDENOSAUNEE INVOLVEMENT IN THE AMERICAN REVOLUTION

Native American involvement was crucial to the course of the American Revolution. Native alliances, especially with the Iroquois Confederacy, helped shape the outcome of the war. The war also was crucial for the confederacy, which split for the first time in several hundred years over the issue of whether to support Great Britain or the new United States of America. The Oneida allied with the Americans and assisted George Washington's army with crucial food supplies during its most difficult winter, at Valley Forge. On the other hand, most of the Mohawk and Seneca sided with the British, and the Senecas especially suffered from brutal raids by troops under the command of General John Sullivan. In the words of historian Richard Aquila, writing in *The Iroquois Restoration*, "The American revolution became an Iroquois civil war." Relatives often found themselves fighting each other as the confederacy split its allegiance between the British and the patriots.

The Seneca war chief Cornplanter advocated neutrality, while Joseph Brant, a Mohawk leader, promoted alliance with the British, as did the Seneca Red Jacket. The name "Red Jacket" was a reference to a scarlet coat the British gave him for fighting with them during the war. Cornplanter insisted that the quarrel was among the whites and that to interfere in something that the Haudenosaunee did not fully understand would be a mistake. Brant contended that neutrality might cause the Iroquois to be attacked by one side without allies on the other. Brant had visited England, acquired a taste for English food and clothes, and been told that the British would return land to the Mohawk in exchange for alliance.

As the meeting broke up in a furor, Brant called Cornplanter a coward. Brant was influential in recruiting many among the Mohawk, Seneca, Cayuga, and Onondaga to support the British. Brant's ferocity as a warrior was legendary; many settlers who supported the Americans called him "Monster Brant." Differing opinions and actions divided the confederacy. Although Skenandoah asserted the Oneida's official neutrality at the beginning of the American Revolution, he supplied warriors and intelligence to the patriots, as did the Tuscarora.

As Washington's army shivered in the snow at Valley Forge, Skenandoah's Oneida carried corn to the starving troops. Washington later named the Shenandoah Valley of Virginia (the name was anglicized) after the Oneida chief in appreciation of his support. In September 1778, the Oneida supplied a timely warning to residents of German Flats, near Herkimer, New York, that

Red Jacket, a Seneca leader, was a great orator and believed in supporting the British during the American Revolution. Later, when Red Jacket met George Washington during negotiations between the Seneca and the new U.S. government, the president gave him an engraved silver medal depicting the two leaders meeting in peace *(above)*.

their settlements were about to be raided by the British and their Iroquois allies under Brant. The settlers were able to get out of the area in time, after which their homes and farms were burned and their livestock captured. The Iroquois also played an important role in the Battle of Oriskany in 1777, the Battle of Wyoming in 1778, and the Battle of Newtown in 1779.

Even as some Iroquois offered lifesaving food to Washington's troops, revolutionary forces often adopted a scorched-earth policy against Haudenosaunee who had allied with the British, or failed to swear allegiance. The war was often very brutal on both sides; Brant's forces torched farms owned by patriots. General Sullivan's raids destroyed much of the Seneca country, with much suffering inflicted on civilians. The toll included 60 villages and their farm fields; the raids, ordered by Washington himself as "chastisement" and "the rod or correction," were carried out with uncommon cruelty, as some soldiers bashed infants' skulls against trees, rationalizing their behavior as "nits make lice." Their economy destroyed, the Seneca suffered disease and hunger for years afterward.

Washington's forces ended the battle for the Mohawk Valley by defeating the British and their Iroquois allies at the Battle of Johnstown in 1781. Following the war, the Brant family and many other Mohawk who supported the British in the revolution moved to Canada to escape retribution by the victorious patriots. They founded the town of Brantford, Ontario, and established a new Haudenosaunee council fire there.

British general Charles Cornwallis surrendered at Yorktown in 1781, but war parties continued to clash along the frontier for months after the British defeat became obvious. The Iroquois allies of the British sent out war parties as late as the early summer of 1782. The Iroquois wanted to continue fighting, but their sponsors had given up. After the war, the efforts of the Iroquois went unrewarded by both sides. The British discarded their Mohawk, Onondaga, Cayuga, and Seneca allies at the earliest convenience.

The Americans did the same to their own allies, the Tuscarora and Oneida. At the conclusion of the Revolutionary War, the border between the new United States and Canada (which remained under British control) was drawn through Iroquois country in the Treaty of Paris (1783), without consultation. At two treaty councils held at Fort Stanwix, New York, many Iroquois realized that the new government was ignoring most of their land claims.

Most of the negotiations were held at gunpoint, as the Iroquois were forced to give up claims to much of their ancestral territories.

THE FORT STANWIX TREATY (1784) AND CANANDAIGUA (PICKERING) TREATY OF 1794

The Treaty of Paris, which outlined the terms of peace between Great Britain and the United States after the Revolutionary War, failed to mention the rights of the British government's Native American allies who remained in the United States. To address this issue, the Indian Committee of the Continental Congress submitted a report to Congress in the fall of 1783 urging that the terms of peace include a demand that the Indians surrender part of their country to the United States without compensation. The New York Assembly proposed to expel all the Mohawk, Onondaga, Cayuga, and Seneca—the nations whose warriors had fought mostly for the British cause—from New York State. Even the Tuscarora and Oneida peoples, who had supported the American cause, were to be exiled to Seneca lands that would be vacated in Western New York under this plan.

United States officials met with representatives of the Six Nations at Fort Stanwix and became very aggressive and insulting, even demanding hostages from the Indians. They insisted on land cessions that the Iroquois delegates had not been empowered to grant and maintained that the Indians as a conquered people had forfeited rights to their lands.

Contrary to Haudenosaunee law and custom, the Indian representatives included very few peace chiefs. The Iroquois' side of the negotiations was primarily conducted by "warriors" who made land cessions, including lands along Lake Erie in Pennsylvania and Ohio that were not authorized by their national councils. When the treaty was submitted to the Six Nations' Grand Council, its terms were rejected. During the treaty talks, Cornplanter, the spokesman for the warriors, separately negotiated a land cession with Pennsylvania that left him with land south of the New York border and a pension. Red Jacket later used this information to destroy Cornplanter's reputation among the Seneca.

The major purpose of the Canandaigua (Pickering) Treaty of 1794 was the establishment of a commission to formalize the border between the United States and Canada. Part of the treaty upholds the right of the Mohawk and other Haudenosaunee peoples to pass freely between the two nations, a right that is still invoked today.

The century of revolutions also took place as new political structures evolved. Benjamin Franklin and other founders of the United States absorbed Iroquois ideas of political structure and ideas of political liberty, mixing them with their European heritage.

Iroquois Ideas and Democracy

In addition to well-known European precedents (Greek and Roman, as well as English common law, among others), indigenous American ideas of democracy have shaped United States government. The immigrants arrived seeking freedom and found it in the confederacies of the Iroquois and other Native nations. By the time of the Constitutional Convention, these ideas were common currency in the former colonies, illustrated in debates involving Benjamin Franklin, Thomas Jefferson, and John Adams. Later, during the nineteenth century, conceptions of Iroquois gender relations

(Opposite map) The Mohawk Trail is one of the earliest and most well-known trade and transportation routes in the 1800s. Established years before any European ship reached North American shores, this route extended from the coast of Massachusetts all the way out towards Michigan. It was later upgraded to accommodate automobiles and was used as a route for the Erie Canal.

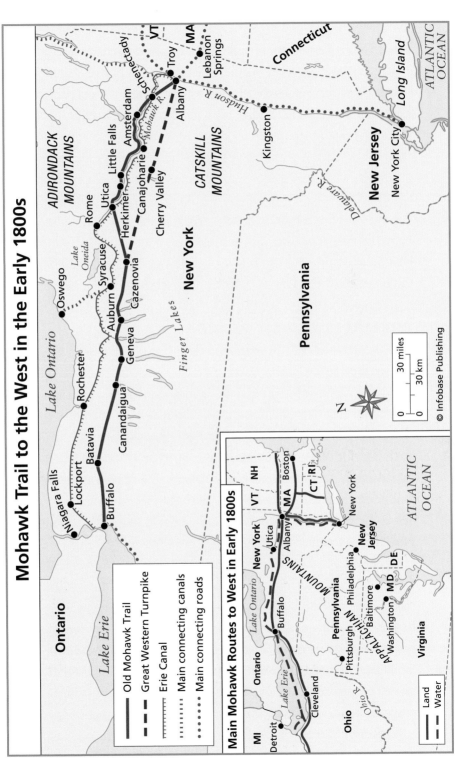

Mohawk Trail to the West in the Early 1800s

Old Mohawk Trail
Great Western Turnpike
Erie Canal
Main connecting canals
Main connecting roads

Main Mohawk Routes to West in Early 1800s

Land
Water

© Infobase Publishing

had an important impact on the major architects of American feminism. These ideas continue to illuminate political debates today.

Throughout eastern North America, many Native American nations had formed confederacies by the time they encountered European immigrants, from the Cherokee and Choctaw in the Carolinas, to the Iroquois in upstate New York and the Wyandot (Huron) near the eastern Great Lakes. The Iroquois system of confederation was the best known to the colonists, in large part because the Iroquois occupied an important position in trade and diplomacy between the English and French colonies, and also among other native peoples. The Iroquois controlled the only relatively level land pass between the English colonies on the seaboard and the French settlements in the St. Lawrence Valley, the later route of the Erie Canal.

THE GREAT LAW OF PEACE

The Haudenosaunee's fundamental law, the Great Law of Peace, stipulates to this day that sachems' skins must be thick to withstand the criticism of the people whom they represent. The law points out that sachems should be careful not to become angry when people scrutinize their conduct in governmental affairs. Such a point of view pervades the writings of Thomas Jefferson and Benjamin Franklin, although it was not fully codified into United States law until the Supreme Court decision in *New York Times Co. v. Sullivan* (1964) made it nearly impossible for public officials to sue successfully for libel.

The Great Law of Peace also provides for the removal of leaders from office who can no longer adequately perform their duties, a measure remarkably similar to a constitutional amendment adopted in the United States during the late twentieth century providing for the removal of an incapacitated president. The Great Law also includes provisions guaranteeing freedom of religion and the right of redress before the Grand Council. It also forbids unauthorized entry of homes—all familiar measures to United States citizens.

The procedure for debating policies in the confederacy begins with the Mohawk and Seneca (the Mohawk, Seneca, and Onondaga are called the "elder brothers"). After being debated by the Keepers of the Eastern Door (Mohawk) and the Keepers of the Western Door (Seneca), the question is then thrown "across the fire" to the Oneida and Cayuga statesmen (the "younger brothers") for discussion in much the same manner. Once consensus is achieved among the Oneida and the Cayuga, the discussion returns to the Seneca and Mohawk for confirmation. Next, the question is laid before the Onondaga, who try to resolve any conflicts that may remain.

At this stage, the Onondaga exercise a power similar to judicial review, as well as the functions built into conference committees in the United States Congress. They can raise objections about the proposal if it is believed to be inconsistent with the Great Law. Essentially, the legislature can rewrite the proposed law on the spot so that it can be in accord with the constitution of the Iroquois. When the Onondaga reach consensus, the Tadadaho, (the speaker of the Grand Council) confirms the decision. This process reflects the emphasis on checks and balances, public debate, and consensus. The overall intent of such a parliamentary procedure is to encourage consensus at each step.

FRANKLIN AS AN INTERCULTURAL LINK

As a printer, Benjamin Franklin published accounts of American Indian treaties for more than two decades. Franklin began his diplomatic career by representing the colony of Pennsylvania at councils with the Iroquois and their allies. His designs for the Albany Plan of Union in 1754 and later the Articles of Confederation contain elements of the Native American systems of confederation that he had come to know as a diplomat.

Born in Boston, Franklin worked with his brother James as a printer until the age of 17. In 1723, he left Massachusetts for Philadelphia, where he became a successful printer and made his mark on history as an inventor, statesman, and philosopher. Franklin's earliest contacts with the Iroquois occurred in Philadelphia, where his printing company published the Indian treaties ratified by the colonial Pennsylvania Assembly.

In 1744, at the Lancaster Treaty Council, Canassatego, an Onondaga sachem and Tadadaho, urged the colonies to unite in a manner similar to that of the Iroquois Confederacy:

> Our wise forefathers established Union and Amity between the Five Nations. This has made us formidable; this has given us great Weight and Authority with our neighboring Nations. We are a powerful Confederacy; and by your observing the same methods our wise forefathers have taken, you will acquire such Strength and power. Therefore whatever befalls you, never fall out with one another.

Franklin probably first learned of Canassatego's advice to the colonies as he set his words in type. Franklin's press issued Indian treaties in small booklets that enjoyed a lively sale throughout the colonies, from 1736 to 1762.

Even before the Albany Congress (the first attempt to unify the colonies), Franklin had been considering the words of Canassatego. Using Iroquois examples of unity, Franklin sought to shame the reluctant colonists into a union in 1751. The word "savages" was not used with disrespect. At the time, it stemmed from a French word that meant "people of the forest." Franklin was being ironic. Actually, Franklin had a great deal of respect for the Iroquois when he said, in a letter to James Parker:

> It would be a strange thing . . . if Six Nations of Ignorant savages should be capable of forming such an union and be able to execute it in such a manner that it has subsisted ages and appears indissoluble [permanent], and yet that a like union should be impractical for ten or a dozen English colonies, to whom it is more necessary and must be more advantageous.

At the Albany Congress in 1754, Franklin outlined a plan for colonial government and union that was the first blueprint for American government and intercolonial unity. His Albany Plan of Union contained elements of English political structure, combined with Haudenosaunee precedents. On July 10, 1754, Franklin

As a printer and a statesman, Benjamin Franklin *(above, seated)* was often asked to print the Native American treaties and agreements and later served as a representative for Pennsylvania at official Iroquois councils. Franklin observed how the Iroquois remained united and believed the colonies should do the same.

formally proposed his Plan of Union before the Albany Congress. Franklin wrote in a personal letter that the debates on the Albany Plan "... went on daily, hand in hand with the Indian business." The Iroquois sachem Hendrick not only spoke for the roughly

200 American Indians in attendance at the congress, but he also briefed the colonial delegates on Iroquois political systems much as Canassatego had done 10 years earlier.

Hendrick was openly critical of the British at the Albany Congress and hinted that the Iroquois would not ally with the English colonies unless a suitable form of unity was established among them. In talking of the proposed union of the colonies and the Six Nations on July 9, 1754, Hendrick stated, according to the treaty record, that "we wish this Tree of Friendship may grow up to a great height and then we shall be a powerful people." Hendrick followed that admonition with an analysis of Iroquois and colonial unity, saying, "We the United Nations shall rejoice of our strength . . . and . . . we have now made so strong a Confederacy." In reply to Hendrick's speech, New York Colonial Governor James DeLancey said: "I hope that by this present Union, we shall grow up to a great height and be as powerful and famous as you were of old."

In drawing up his final draft of the Albany Plan for colonial unification, Franklin was meeting several diplomatic demands: the British government's for control, the colonies' desires for autonomy in a loose confederation, and the Iroquois' stated advocacy for a colonial union similar (but not identical) to their own. For the Crown, the plan provided administration by a president general, to be appointed by England. The individual colonies were to be allowed to retain their own constitutions, except as the plan limited them. The retention of internal sovereignty within the individual colonies closely resembled the Iroquois system and had no existing precedent in Europe.

Franklin used his image of Indians and their societies as a critique of Europe:

> The Care and Labour of providing for Artificial and fashionable Wants, the sight of so many Rich wallowing in superfluous plenty, while so many are kept poor and distress'd for want; the Insolence of Office . . . [and] restraints of Custom, all contrive to disgust them [Indians] with what we call civil Society.

Franklin described the Indians' passion for liberty while making it a patriotic rallying cry; he admired Indians' notions of happiness while seeking a definition that would suit the new nation. Franklin wrote:

> All the Indians of North America not under the dominion of the Spaniards are in that natural state, being restrained by no Laws, having no Courts, or Ministers of Justice, no Suits, no prisons, no governors vested with any Legal Authority. The persuasion of Men distinguished by Reputation of Wisdom is the only Means by which others are govern'd, or rather led—and the State of the Indians was probably the first State of all Nations.

As U.S. ambassador to France, among the French *philosophes*, Franklin was known as the "Philosopher as Savage." In his essay "Remarks Concerning the Savages of North America," Franklin asserted that Indians should not be regarded as uncivilized. Although sometimes paradoxical in his outlook, Franklin often compared the virtues and shortcomings of both Indian and white cultures, asserting that Indian ideas and customs had great wisdom and value.

THOMAS JEFFERSON AND NATIVE AMERICAN CONCEPTS OF GOVERNMENT

While Benjamin Franklin and Thomas Jefferson were too pragmatic to believe that they could copy the "natural state," its image was incorporated early into the United States' ideas of freedom. Jefferson, the primary author of the Declaration of Independence (Franklin was his editor), said that "the only condition on earth to be compared with ours, in my opinion, is that of the Indian, where they have still less law than we." When Thomas Paine wrote (on the first page of *Common Sense*) that "government, like dress, is the badge of lost innocence," he was recapitulating observations of Native American societies directly, or through the eyes of European philosophers such as John Locke and Jean-Jacques Rousseau. *Common Sense* was a popular booklet by Paine, the revolution's best-known agitator, that advocated freedom for the British colonies, spurring the American Revolution.

In 1787, in a letter to Edward Carrington (a Virginia delegate to the Continental Congress between 1786 and 1788), Jefferson associated freedom of expression with public opinion as well as happiness, citing American Indian societies as an example:

> The basis of our government being the opinion of the people, our very first object should be to keep that right; and were it left to me to decide whether we should have a government without newspapers or newspapers without a government, I should not hesitate for a moment to prefer the latter. . . . I am convinced that those societies [as the Indians] which live without government enjoy in their general mass an infinitely greater degree of happiness than those who live under European governments.

"Without government" could not have meant without social order to Jefferson. He, Franklin, and Paine all knew Native societies too well to argue that they functioned without social order, in the classic "noble savage" image as wild men of the woods. It was clear that the Iroquois, for example, did not organize a confederacy with alliances spreading over much of Northeastern North America "without government." They did it, however, with a non-European conception of government, of which Jefferson, Paine, and Franklin were appreciative students who sought to factor "natural law" and "natural rights" into their designs for the United States.

A DEBATE REGARDING FEDERALISM AT THE CONSTITUTIONAL CONVENTION

By June 1787, the delegates to the Constitutional Convention were engaged in a debate about the fundamental nature of United States government. Many delegates appeared to agree with James Wilson when he stated, on June 1, 1787, that he would not be "governed by the British model which was inapplicable to . . . this country."

(continues on page 69)

Native American Ideas and the Origins of American Feminism

The influential role of women in the political life of the Iroquois and other Native American societies intrigued, perplexed, and sometimes alarmed European and European-American observers (nearly all of whom were men) during the seventeenth and eighteenth centuries. In many cases women then and now held and hold pivotal positions in Native political systems. Iroquois clan mothers, for example, nominate men to positions of lead-

Matilda Joslyn Gage was a suffragist fighting for equal rights in New York. Her writing references how Iroquois women were relied on to make effective and powerful decisions.

ership and can "dehorn," or impeach, them for misconduct. Women often have veto power over men's plans for war. In a matrilineal society (and nearly all the confederacies that bordered the early United States were matrilineal), women owned all household goods except the men's clothes, weapons, and hunting implements. They also were the primary conduits of culture from generation to generation.

Pressure to broaden the scope of natural and civil rights for women arose early in the nineteenth century at roughly the same time as the abolitionist movement against slavery intensified. While the landmark Seneca Falls conference,

(continues)

(continued)

which is usually credited with beginning the modern feminist movement in the United States, was not held until 1848, the ideological basis for the movement was set down by Lydia Maria Child in her *History of the Condition of Women, in Various Ages and Nations*, published in 1835. Child's book used the Iroquois and Wyandot (Huron) cultures to counterpoise the dominant model of European patriarchy, illustrating the importance of Native American women in political decision making. Child's work was extensively used by later suffragists, including Matilda Joslyn Gage and Elizabeth Cady Stanton, both of whom cited Iroquois society as an example of equality in gender relations. With Stanton and Susan B. Anthony, Gage cowrote the landmark *History of Woman Suffrage*.

Iroquois women were very influential as clan mothers, and they chose the leaders. The men filled the public roles, and so are recognized in history. Thus a paradox: While Iroquois women maintained behind-the-scenes influence, it was collective and anonymous. There was little personal presence in history.

The role of women in Iroquois society helped inspire some of the most influential advocates of modern feminism in the United States. The Iroquois example figures importantly in Gage's *Woman, Church and State* (1893), a valuable book written during what Sally R. Wagner calls the first wave of feminism. In her book, Gage acknowledges, according to Wagner's research, that "the modern world [is] indebted [to the Iroquois] for its first conception of inherent rights, natural equality of condition, and the establishment of a civilized government upon this basis."

Gage was one of the nineteenth century's three most influential feminists, along with Stanton and Anthony. Gage herself was admitted to the Iroquois Council of Matrons and was adopted into the Wolf Clan, with the name *Karonienhawi*, "she who holds [up] the sky."

(continued from page 66)

Wilson believed that America's size was so great, and its ideals so "republican, that nothing but a great confederated republic would do for it." A signer of the Declaration of Independence, Wilson was later elected to the Continental Congress and was an important figure in debates over the U.S. Constitution. He also was one of the first justices appointed by President George Washington to the U.S. Supreme Court.

In 1787, on the eve of the Constitutional Convention, John Adams published his *Defence of the Constitutions of Government of the United States of America*. Although Adams was selected as a Massachusetts delegate to the Constitutional Convention, he chose not to attend and published his lengthy essay instead. Adams's *Defence* was a critical survey of world governments that included a description of the Iroquois and other Native American governments, as well as many other historical examples of confederacies in Europe and Asia.

Defence was not an endorsement of Native models for government. Instead, Adams refuted the arguments of Franklin, who advocated a one-house legislature resembling the Iroquois Grand Council, a model that had been used in the Albany Plan and Articles of Confederation. Adams did not trust the consensus model that seemed to work for the Iroquois. He believed that, without the checks and balances built into two legislative houses, the system would fall to control by special interests and dissolve into anarchy or despotism (dictatorship). When Adams described the Mohawk's independence, he was expressing criticism, while Franklin wrote about Indian governments in a much more approving way.

As the Iroquois shaped the thinking of the United States' founders, immigrants were moving into their lands and defrauding them. The same Iroquois whose ideas had been so appealing to some European-Americans found themselves fighting assimilation.

Battling Land Loss and Assimilation

After 1800, the Iroquois Confederacy, like most Native Americans, faced a long struggle against destruction of their land bases, cultures, and livelihoods. These struggles also spawned revival movements, the most important of which was the Code of Handsome Lake. The Haudenosaunee successfully resisted removal westward for the most part, but at the same time they lost very large amounts of their homelands. Against all odds, some Iroquois became prominent in American society.

FRAUDULENT LOSSES OF LAND

From 1784 to 1838, much of the Haudenosaunee nations' land holdings were taken through fraudulent treaty claims; many of these were illegal because they violated the various nonintercourse acts passed by Congress during the same period. Nonintercourse acts prohibited the sale of Indian land without the approval of

Congress. They were meant to prohibit cheating in dealings involving land. As a result of these land cessions, some Haudenosaunee people moved to Canada (to Grand River and other communities), Wisconsin, Kansas, and Indian Territory (later Oklahoma). A sizable Oneida reservation has become one of the largest employers in Green Bay, Wisconsin, but most of the other settlements are small.

None of the treaties were approved by the Haudenosaunee Grand Council. Usually, a wealthy land speculator would ask the state legislature to authorize a treaty or agreement with an Indian nation from which the speculator wished to extract land. The legislature would then authorize the agreement and find some members of the nation (who were usually not authorized to act by its people as a whole) to sign a treaty. These "treaty chiefs" would then be bribed to concede, or give up, property, usually for a fraction of what the land would have been worth on the open market.

Another device was the lease-as-sale. The Indians would be told that they were signing a lease, when actually they were signing to sell their land. Most of western New York State changed hands by one of these two methods. Such land transfers were probably in violation of the Fort Stanwix Treaty of 1784, which recognizes the Haudenosaunee's jurisdiction over their aboriginal lands. These devices also violated the federal nonintercourse acts passed between 1790 and 1834, which were meant to prevent just this kind of fraud.

THE BUFFALO CREEK TREATIES (1838, 1842)

The Buffalo Creek Treaty of 1838 was one of the worst government-assisted land frauds in United States history. Lewis Henry Morgan, whose *League of the Haudenosaunee* was published barely more than a decade after the Buffalo Creek Treaty was executed, said in that book that the treaty was carried out "with a degree of wickedness hardly to be paralleled in the history of human avarice."

In January 1838, the Seneca, under protest, sold their four remaining reservations (at Allegany, Cattaraugus, Tonawanda, and Buffalo Creek) to the Ogden Land Company, with a representative of the United States in attendance. For their 202,000 acres (81,746 hectares) in New York State, the Indians (mostly Senecas) were paid $202,000 ($1 an acre). The Senecas fought this plan bitterly. Despite revelations of fraud, forgery, and bribery on the part of Ogden Land Company's negotiators, Congress ratified the treaty under pressure from President Andrew Jackson, who favored Indian removals.

The Revival of Handsome Lake (Sganyadaí:yoh)

Even as the Iroquois were losing much of their land, a revival movement began in a religious context. Handsome Lake, a Seneca, provided a code of conduct that is still widely followed today. *Sganyadaí:yoh*, his Seneca name, means "beautiful" (i.e., handsome) lake, a reference to Lake Ontario. The term is not a personal name, but a Seneca position title on the Haudenosaunee Grand Council.

Sganyadaí:yoh was a visionary and spiritual leader who established the Longhouse Religion among the New York Iroquois in the early nineteenth century. *Gaiwí:yo*, the Code of Handsome Lake, a repository of his visions and ethical teachings, borrowed heavily from Christianity to conserve traditional ways then being suppressed by the Euro-American government, which often allowed church officials to run the New York reservations.

A half-century after his death, elders called a council to gather his words, which Keepers (who maintained oral history) committed to memory and knotted into wampum. Sganyadaí:yoh had himself knotted wampum of his *Gaiwí:yo*. He began to be called *Sedwa´gowa´ne*, meaning "our great teacher." In 1848, a recital of the *Gaiwí:yo* by *Sos´heowa* was taken down on paper for the first time at a mourning council in Tonawanda and translated for Lewis Henry Morgan by *Donehogä´wa* (Ely S. Parker).

In 1842, in another treaty negotiation, also at Buffalo Creek, the Allegany and Tonawanda reservations were returned to the Seneca, but the Ogden Land Company retained preemption rights, which establish legal superiority against other claims.

In 1857, however, the Tonawanda Seneca were allowed to repurchase part of the land sold to the Ogden Land Company almost two decades earlier.

In 1851, it was published in Morgan's book, *The League of the Haudenosaunee*. Ten years later, the Grand Council accepted the Gaiwí:yo as legitimate. At the turn of the twentieth century, *Gawaso Wanneh* (Arthur Caswell Parker), a descendant of *Sganyadaí:yoh*, published another transcription. In 1994, Chief Jacob Thomas provided yet another version of the code.

Between the death of *Sganyadaí:yoh* in 1815 and 1900, the Longhouse Religion flowered, gathering many supporters. By the turn of the twen-

Handsome Lake *(above, with cane)*, a Seneca leader, developed "the Longhouse Religion," to provide a code that would allow the Iroquois to return to their traditional beliefs.

tieth century, a low point for all Native American groups, Arthur Parker observed that the teachings of *Sganyadaí:yoh* were on the wane and that "true believers" numbered only a few hundred. By the mid-twentieth century, however, the *Gaiwí:yo* was being recited with great frequency on the New York reservations and, with the general Native renaissance of the 1970s, many young New York Haudenosaunee began to look into it as a way to trace their roots. Today, "The Longhouse Religion," as it is often called, is practiced in most Iroquois communities.

COLONEL ELY PARKER (*DONEHOGÄ´WA*) SENECA: U.S. INDIAN COMMISSIONER

Amid constant pressure against their land, culture, and identity, the Iroquois distinguished themselves in what was a very tough time to be Native American. One example was Colonel Ely Parker (Donehogä´wa), who was secretary to General (and later U.S. president) Ulysses S. Grant. Parker wrote the surrender terms ending the Civil War that General Robert E. Lee signed at Appomattox. After the Civil War, Parker became the first Native American commissioner of Indian Affairs after Grant was elected president.

Parker had planned a legal career. He passed the necessary examinations but was denied certification because he was American Indian and therefore, at the time, not a U.S. citizen. Parker switched to civil engineering. He also acquired a considerable background in ethnology (a discipline within anthropology that analyzes various groups, or ethnicities, of human beings). Parker also helped to inspire Lewis Henry Morgan's pioneering studies of the Iroquois that founded academic anthropology in the United States. Parker became an early member of the Grand Order of the Iroquois, a fraternal society started by Morgan.

Parker's tenure in the Bureau of Indian Affairs coincided with investigations of corruption on the frontier by Congress under Senator James B. Doolittle. The Doolittle Report received considerable publicity, finding that, in a large number of cases, Indian wars could be traced to European-Americans who had seized Native lands illegally after violating treaty terms. Parker came into office under a peace policy initiated by Congress after publicity surrounding the Doolittle Report, in an attempt to deal honestly with surviving Native American nations. However, the Indian Rings, whose members had done so much to corrupt the system and profited so handsomely from government contracts for services paid but rarely delivered, made Parker's life miserable and his job impossible.

During Parker's tenure as Indian Affairs commissioner, however, he helped orchestrate considerable public outrage over the treatment of Native people nationwide, particularly those on

Ely Parker, a Seneca, drew up the agreement between generals Ulysses S. Grant and Robert E. Lee at the end of the Civil War. Hoping to become a lawyer, Parker was denied the opportunity because he was Native American. Instead, he went to work for Grant as the head of the Bureau of Indian Affairs.

the Plains, who were being ruthlessly pursued as he served in the office. After Parker was hounded out of office, he expressed his disgust. He was quoted in Peter Nabokov's *Native American Testimony* (1991) as having said: "They made their onslaught on my poor, innocent head and made the air foul with their malicious and poisonous accusations. They were defeated, but it was no longer a pleasure to discharge patriotic duties in the face of foul slander and abuse. I gave up a thankless position to enjoy my declining years in peace and quiet."

Asserting Ancient Rights

In the twentieth century, the Iroquois found their land base reduced and their culture threatened, but with the aid of group effort and some remarkable people, they struggled to preserve land and culture. Deskaheh (Levi General) took the Iroquois case to the League of Nations, as Arthur Caswell Parker, a prolific author, blazed a trail in the museum world. Land loss was still an issue, however, as Cornplanter's descendants saw their land submerged behind the Kinzua Dam in the 1960s, and the Oneida pursued a large land claim. Later, Leon Shenandoah served as Tadadaho of the Iroquois Confederacy and took his people's affairs before a world audience again, this time at the United Nations. The Iroquois again exercised their sovereignty in World War II, when some of them volunteered for service after the Longhouse declared war. They also defended border-crossing rights between the United States and Canada.

A SENECA IN THE MUSEUM WORLD

Arthur C. Parker (whose Iroquois name *Gawaso Wanneh* means "Big Snowsnake") became one of history's leading Native Americans in anthropology and museum directorship, as well as a prolific author. Parker also brought the word *museologist* into the English language. He was the longtime curator at the Rochester Municipal Museum, later known as the Rochester Museum and Science Center. He also was involved in the Society of American Indians, an early pan-Indian group that pressed for reform of policy toward Native Americans nationwide. He was the group's first secretary at its initial meeting in 1911, advocating a platform "to encourage Indian leadership, promote self-help, and foster the assimilation of Indians while encouraging them to exhibit pride in their race."

Born on the Cattaraugus Seneca reservation on April 5, 1881, the one-quarter-blood Parker was a great-nephew of Ely S. Parker, secretary to Ulysses S. Grant during the Civil War, as well as a distant relative of the Iroquois prophet Handsome Lake. After studying at Dickinson Seminary in Pennsylvania, Parker came to know Dr. Frederick Ward Putnam, a leading museum director, while studying at Harvard.

Parker never finished his degree at Harvard, but he became a field archaeologist for Harvard's Peabody Museum in 1903. Parker also worked part time at the American Museum of Natural History before he was appointed state archaeologist for the New York State Museum in Albany in 1906. Parker took the lead in excavating several Iroquois sites and organized the New York State Archaeological Survey as he built the State Museum into a major center for archaeological study. In the meantime, Parker also authored *The Archaeological History of New York*.

In 1925, Parker was appointed director of the Rochester Municipal Museum, a role that he held for almost two decades. While Parker was best known as a museum director, he was also a prolific author. He wrote roughly 500 pieces during his lifetime, ranging from books to journal and magazine articles (published and not), radio scripts, plays, and other works. His personal bibliography eventually included 14 books, among them *Erie Indian Village* (1913), *Code of Handsome Lake* (1913), *Life of General Ely S. Parker* (1919), *Seneca Myths and Folk Tales* (1923), and *Last of the Senecas* (1952).

Joy Porter's *To Be Indian* (2001), the first full-scale biography of Parker, brings him to life:

> Although not tall, at perhaps five feet six inches, he cut a dignified figure in his smart clothes with his dark hair and hazel eyes winking out from under his trademark fedora. Some thought he looked quintessentially "Indian"; others thought of him as "white." However they encountered him, people seem to have warmed to Parker because of his skill at putting them at ease. A lover of puns and word games, he was friendly, with a charming sense of humor.

Parker was known for popular innovation in museums, which he called "the university of the common man." He worked to make exhibits more interactive and appealing to a broad range of people. On his death in 1955, Parker was recalled very warmly by Ray Fadden, who wrote that "the Chief," as he was often called, "was a great person, desiring nothing for himself, quiet, ever watching, and ever ready to do good for everyone, no matter who." Obscuring his earlier doubts about Native American cultural survival and his eugenic ruminations, Parker's affectionate personality won out in the end—a tribute to his essential humanity.

PETITIONING THE LEAGUE OF NATIONS FOR IROQUOIS RIGHTS

While Arthur Parker worked in the museum world, the Cayuga Deskaheh (Levi General), Tadadaho (speaker) of the Iroquois Grand Council at Grand River, Ontario, during the early 1920s, sought diplomatic recognition for the Iroquois on the world stage.

During Deskaheh's time Canadian authorities closed the traditional Longhouse, which had been asserting independence from Canadian jurisdiction. Canadian authorities proposed to set up a governmental structure that would answer to the country's Indian-affairs bureaucracy. With Canadian police about to arrest him, Deskaheh traveled to the headquarters of the League of Nations in Geneva, Switzerland, carrying a Haudenosaunee passport, with an appeal for support from the international community.

Several months of effort did not win Deskaheh a hearing before the international body, in large part because of diplomatic manipulation by Great Britain and Canada, governments that were being embarrassed by Deskaheh's mission. Lacking a forum at the League of Nations, Deskaheh and his supporters organized a private meeting in Switzerland that drew several thousand people supporting Iroquois sovereignty.

In his last speech, on March 10, 1925, Deskaheh, according to an account published by the Six Nations Indian Museum of Onchiota, New York, had lost none of his distaste for forced assimilation. "Over in Ottawa, they call that policy 'Indian Advancement,'" he said. "Over in Washington, they call it 'Assimilation.' We who would be the helpless victims say it is tyranny.... If this must go on to the bitter end, we would rather that you come with your guns and poison gas and get rid of us that way. Do it openly and above board."

As he was dying, relatives of Deskaheh who lived in the United States were refused entry into Canada to be at his bedside. Deskaheh died two-and-a-half months after his last defiant speech. Many Iroquois have maintained his notions of sovereignty into contemporary times. The Iroquois Grand Council at Onondaga issues its own passports, which are recognized by Switzerland and several other countries, but not by the United States or Canada.

THE IROQUOIS IN WORLD WAR II

Many Iroquois shared Deskaheh's beliefs in national sovereignty. In an expression of sovereignty, many Iroquois refused to serve in

World War II until the Grand Council had declared war on Japan and Germany. One of the signature cases in this effort involved Ernest Benedict, who volunteered for military service in World War II, after objecting to the draft in peacetime on the grounds that the United States could not conscript Haudenosaunee to enlist in its armed forces. Benedict initially served three months in jail for refusing to be drafted because he could not afford even minimal bail. He later volunteered for service to avoid further prosecution and because war had been declared following Japan's attack on Pearl Harbor. Eleanor Roosevelt intervened with local Selective Service authorities to allow Benedict's release from jail.

Another case involved Warren Green, whose mother argued in *Ex Parte Green* that he was not a U.S. citizen. The case was filed on behalf of Iroquois leaders, who sought Green's release from military duty on a writ of habeas corpus. The writ was denied in district court, after which Green appealed to the U.S. Court of Appeals for the Second Circuit. This court ruled against Green in November 1941, asserting that the Citizenship Act of 1924, backed by the Nationality Act of 1940, made American Indians citizens of the United States.

The judges in the appeals court did express doubts, however. Judge Thomas Swan, cited in Paul Rosier's *Serving Their Country: American Indian Politics and Patriotism in the Twentieth Century* (2009), said, "The white men have treated Indians shabbily for so long that I would like to give them a break on compulsory military service, but I don't see how we can work it out in any lawyer-like way." Judge Jerome Frank said that the three judges of the appeals court had "taxed [their] ingenuity in vain to find any interpretation which would result in a decision in [Green's] favor." Green, like Benedict, was not objecting to military service itself but asserting the Iroquois' right to a status as a nation within a nation.

CORNPLANTER, CAN YOU SWIM?

During the 1950s and 1960s, the Haudenosaunee lost several thousand acres of land to dams, reservoirs, highways, electrical and gas lines, and waterways. These losses occurred during a time

The Kinzua Dam in Pennsylvania was built to help meet the growing demand for electricity. The resulting effect was not only more electricity, but also the destruction of Seneca land that had existed for generations. After the dam was built, the subsequent flooding of Seneca territory was said to have destroyed Handsome Lake's grave.

when many Indian peoples were losing their land in a legislative process called Termination. The best-known Iroquois example of such land seizures (usually under governmental agency powers allowing seizure of land for "eminent domain," or public uses) was the Kinzua Dam, which flooded land promised to the Seneca in an agreement between George Washington and Cornplanter.

Cornplanter's people occupied the piece of land along the Allegheny River until the mid-twentieth century, when the Army Corps of Engineers decided that a dam was needed on the river. The scope of the Army's engineering projects had grown grandiosely since Washington himself helped survey the mountains that now comprise West Virginia, long before the generation of electricity became a legally valid reason for the state to seize land.

In August 1941, Congress authorized the Allegheny Reservoir Project. World War II intervened, so the project was not officially taken up again until 1956. The dam was to be built at the Kinzua narrows along the Allegheny River just to the south of New York's border with Pennsylvania. The Seneca reservation was 12 miles (19 kilometers) downstream. The dam, which cost $125 million, flooded all Seneca land below 1,365 feet (416 meters) in elevation, including the entire Cornplanter Tract. The Seneca fought proposals to build a dam since 1927 using the Canandaigua Treaty as a defense, only to be told by the federal courts in 1958 that the "plenary power" of Congress allowed it to abrogate treaties unilaterally. The U.S. Supreme Court validated that point of view in June 1959 by denying the Seneca a writ of *certiorari*.

The construction of the Kinzua Dam flooded one-third of the Allegany Seneca reservation, in violation of the Canandaigua Treaty. The dam flooded 9,000 acres of Seneca land on the reservation, requiring the removal of about 160 families, or about 600 people, from the valley in which many of them had lived for several generations. Seneca G. Peter Jemison recalled that "our elders wept openly, and as a result of that, we lost many of them [to death] in the succeeding years." In 1964, the bones of Cornplanter's people were moved from their land to make way for rising waters behind the Kinzua Dam. In the valleys at the Western Door, Seneca still wonder sardonically if George Washington had ever asked Cornplanter if he knew how to swim.

Peter La Farge, a Native American poet and musician, described the eviction of the Seneca in a ballad, "As Long As the Grass Shall Grow," which became the first song on Johnny Cash's 1964 album, *Bitter Tears*. Released at the height of the folk music revival in the United States, Cash's album was refused airtime by many radio stations because it graphically portrayed hardships faced by Native Americans. Thus, the album failed to sell well, but it has endured among indigenous people.

A PRELUDE TO "RED POWER" ACTIVISM

In another assertion of sovereignty, Wallace "Mad Bear" Anderson (1927–1985, Tuscarora), a noted Native American rights activist during the 1950s, advocated "Red Power" activism before it spread across North America with the founding of the American Indian Movement during the late 1960s. Anderson later became a spokesman for Native American sovereignty in several international forums. Writer Edmund Wilson recalled Anderson in *Apologies to the Iroquois* as "a young man in a lumberjack shirt and cap, broad of build, with a round face and lively black eyes."

Anderson was born in Buffalo, New York, and raised on the Tuscarora Reservation near Niagara Falls. Anderson's grandmother first used the name "Mad Bear" in reference to his hotheadedness. He adopted the name from her. Anderson served in the U.S. Navy during World War II at Okinawa. He later served in Korea. Anderson became an activist after his request for a GI Bill loan to build a house on the Tuscarora Reservation was rejected.

Anderson led protests against Iroquois payment of New York State income taxes as early as 1957. At the height of the protest, several hundred Akwesasne (St. Regis) Mohawk marched to the state courthouse in Massena, New York, where they burned summonses issued for unpaid taxes. The Iroquois also objected (without success) to the joint United States–Canada construction of the St. Lawrence Seaway because it threatened the land base of the Tuscarora and Mohawk, arguing that a nation within a nation had a legal right to survival.

In 1958, Anderson played a leading role in protests of a 1,383-acre (559.68-ha) seizure of Tuscarora land (of their 6,249-acre, or 2,528.8-ha, reservation) by the New York Power Authority for construction of a dam and reservoir. Anderson and other Iroquois deflated workers' tires and blocked surveyors' transits. When the Tuscarora refused to sell the land, a force of about 100 state troopers and police invaded their reservation. Anderson met the troopers and police with about 150 nonviolent demonstrators who

Noted activist Wallace "Mad Bear" Anderson was the first to practice "Red Power" activism in the United States. Using nonviolent protest, Mad Bear publicized how the government violated longstanding treaty agreements and the injustices done to Native Americans. Above, Mad Bear burns a Supreme Court injunction preventing him and his group from stopping planned construction of a highway through Onondaga territory.

blocked their trucks by lying in the road. The U.S. Supreme Court sided with the state in 1960, citing eminent domain.

During March 1959, Anderson helped compose a declaration of sovereignty at the Iroquois Six Nations Reserve in Brantford, Ontario, the settlement established by Joseph Brant and his followers after the American Revolution. The declaration prompted an occupation of the reserve's Council House by the Royal Canadian Mounted Police. During the same month, Anderson attempted a citizen's arrest of commissioner of Indian Affairs Glen L. Emmons in Washington, D.C., on allegations of misconduct in office. Emmons avoided the intended arrest but later resigned. During July 1959, Anderson traveled to Cuba with a delegation of Iroquois and other Native Americans to exchange recognitions of sovereignty with Fidel Castro, whose revolutionary army had seized power only months earlier.

In 1967, Anderson formed the North American Indian Unity Caravan, which traveled the United States for six years as the types of activism that he had pioneered spread nationwide. Anderson also gathered opposition to Termination legislation from 133 Native American tribes and nations and carried it to Washington, D.C., effectively killing the last attempt to buy out reservations in the United States. In 1969, he helped initiate the takeover of Alcatraz Island in California.

Anderson died in December 1985 after a long illness at age 58 on the Tuscarora Reservation in New York State.

ONEIDA LAND CLAIMS: RIGHTS VS. FACTS

When the United States prohibited the sale of Indian land without federal approval by passing the Trade and Intercourse Acts (beginning in 1790), many states and individuals ignored the laws and bought or seized Native American land anyway. Nearly two centuries later, these laws were brought back into court as Native

(continues on page 88)

Leon Shenandoah: "Waging Peace" on the World Stage

Leon Shenandoah served as Tadadaho of the Iroquois Confederacy during much of the late twentieth century, from his initiation in 1969 until shortly before his death from kidney failure on July 22, 1996, at age 81. Shenandoah, a gentle, soft-spoken, humble man, held the oldest continuous political office in North America and one of the oldest in the world. The Iroquois Confederacy has seated a Tadadaho since at least about 1100. According to Iroquois oral historians, Shenandoah was the 235th Tadadaho of the confederacy.

Shenandoah was a frequent international representative of the confederacy, speaking at the Earth Summit in Brazil in 1992 and, twice, before the United Nations. Speaking at the United Nations in 1985, Shenandoah outlined the principles of Iroquois leadership. Quoting from the Great Law of Peace, he said that the Haudenosaunee chiefs "shall be mentors of the people for all time. The thickness of their skins shall be seven spans, which is to say that they shall be proof against anger, offensive action, and criticism. Their hearts shall be full of peace and goodwill, and their minds full of a yearning for the welfare of the people. With endless patience, they shall carry out their duty. Their firmness shall be tempered with a tenderness for their people. Neither anger nor fury shall find lodging in their minds, and all their words and actions shall be marked by calm deliberation."

Shenandoah called upon world leaders to abolish nuclear and conventional weapons of war. "When warriors are leaders, then you will have war," he said. Leaders must be taught to wage peace, he said. "We must unite the religions of the world as the spiritual force strong enough to prevail in peace. It is no longer good enough to cry, 'Peace.' We must act peace, live peace, and march [for] peace in alliance with the people of the world."

As Tadadaho, Shenandoah was regarded as both a political and a spiritual leader. When asked about Iroquois influences on American democracy, Shenandoah said that the United States' founders made a mistake when they divorced state and church. "When the United States copied our form of government in the 1750s, they left out spirituality," Shenandoah said. "This is what I learned as a child.... Our religion is within the government and our government is within our religion. It is entwined. If the government goes off to one side... the religion will then pull you back in line... [one] counteracts the other.... But when the United States joined the 13 colonies and copied our form of government, they held their meetings in one house, and their church (their beliefs) in another house.... It's not under the same roof like we do."

Shortly after he assumed office, Shenandoah visited the Museum of the American Indian in New York City. Later he told Doug George-Kanentiio that when a receptionist asked, "May I help you," he quietly said, "Yes. You can give us back our wampum belts." For three decades, Shenandoah played an important role in a campaign to have the wampum belts, which are records of the confederacy, returned from several museums and from New York State. His last official act, on July 4, 1996, was to preside over the return of 74 wampum belts from the same museum where he had greeted the receptionist many years earlier. Even though Shenandoah was ailing and had resigned office the previous fall due to illness, he donned his feather hat and assumed his office for the return of these precious belts.

At home, Shenandoah was a quiet, traditionally-minded man who drove an old Pontiac that someone had given to him and smoked a corncob pipe. His modest home was heated with a wood stove, and was situated close to the site of his birth, which occured on May 18, 1915, in a cabin on Hemlock Creek. He was the youngest of five siblings. His schooling had ended at eighth grade. With his wife, Thelma, Shenandoah raised seven children, meanwhile maintaining his fluency in the Onondaga language and his intense interest in Haudenosaunee traditions, including the Code of Handsome Lake.

(continued from page 85)

peoples argued that their land had been illegally seized. In *County of Oneida v. Oneida Indian Nation* (1985), the Oneida people won rights to 100,000 acres (40,468 ha) of land transferred to New York State in 1795, while George Washington was president of the United States.

The case was filed in 1970 and was originally dismissed in federal courts for lack of jurisdiction. The case was contested in the courts until the Supreme Court reversed the lower court decisions during its 1985 session. The court held that the Oneida had a right to sue under common law and that this right had not been diminished by the passage of time because it was not limited by a statute of limitations or any other form of abatement. The court also said that the Oneida had an "unquestioned right" to their lands and that the Indians' right of occupancy was "as sacred as the fee simple of the whites." The court's decision was split 5 to 4, and the case was bitterly contested, because it denied the property rights of some owners who had held title for as long as 175 years.

The court decision was only a first step, however, since much of the land in question had been passed to multiple private owners during the two centuries since it was taken from the Oneida. By 2009, the Oneida had not won a single actual acre under this ruling. Having opened a large casino, the Turning Stone, the Oneida, however, were slowly buying back several thousand acres.

BORDER CROSSING RIGHTS

Because officials in Canada failed to observe the Canandaigua (Pickering) Treaty (1794), Akwesasne Mohawk (whose home straddles the border) blockaded an international bridge in 1968.

Ernest Benedict was active during 1968 in protest of Canadian policies that curtailed Mohawk freedom of movement across the international border, which is guaranteed under this treaty. From their home on Cornwall Island, the Mohawk of Akwesasne prepared to blockade the nearby International Bridge and force the issue of policies that required them to pay customs duties on anything worth more than $5 that crossed the border, including food and other necessities of daily life. More than 100 Mohawk imposed a wall of bodies that stopped traffic; then they let air out of the tires of many stalled vehicles. Police arrested 41 Mohawk. After a second blockade in February 1969 and a long series of negotiations, Canadian officials agreed to abide by the terms of the Pickering Treaty.

Akwesasne leader Mike Mitchell was arrested during the same year for transporting a number of household goods across the border, a case that was revisited after another border crossing in 1988, when Mitchell was charged after refusing to pay duty on goods he took across the border. Mitchell's legal battle regarding interpretation of Iroquois border-crossing rights under the Jay Treaty was still alive in 1997, more than 200 years after the treaty was signed. The Canadian federal government in September 1997 decided to appeal a court ruling that affirmed the Mohawk's border-crossing rights. At issue was the right of the Mohawk to cross the border without paying duty on goods meant to be traded with other Native Americans. In November 1998, Canadian courts upheld the original ruling in support of the Iroquois.

Iroquois in Today's World

As they have throughout their history, the Iroquois today place an important value on their sovereignty. Land claims are being pursued. The Oneida have a claim that has been recognized by the U.S. Supreme Court but never implemented. The Onondaga have a claim that includes most of the city of Syracuse, New York, but do not want to evict anyone. The Mohawk's land claims include large areas near the Canadian border. The Iroquois sense of independent nationhood remains quite strong. Some Iroquois representatives carry passports when they travel on diplomatic business for the Grand Council.

The Iroquois have also taken part in language revitalization and have reclaimed their ancient wampum belts from the State of New York. At the same time, they have engaged in important debates over the appropriate use of their sovereignty for commercial purposes, most notably the sale of tobacco and support of gambling. Many Iroquois oppose the development of casinos. They also face some of the most acute environmental pollution in North America.

TOXICITY AT AKWESASNE

In two generations, the Akwesasne Mohawk's land has become so poisoned that it is not safe to eat the fish or game. In some locations it is not safe even to drink the water, while in others people have been told not to till the soil. Akwesasne has become the most polluted native reserve in Canada and one of the most severely poisoned sections of earth in the United States.

These environmental circumstances have descended on a people whose entire way of life has been enmeshed with the natural world, in a place where the Iroquois origin story says the world took shape on a gigantic turtle's back. Today, environmental pathologists are finding turtles at Akwesasne that qualify as toxic waste.

A once-pristine landscape of rivers and forests has been turned into a chemical dump where unsuspecting children played on piles of dirt laced with polychlorinated biphenyls (PCBs) discarded by a nearby General Motors foundry. PCBs, chemicals used to insulate electrical equipment, were banned by the federal government during the 1970s. In some forms PCBs cause liver damage and several types of cancer.

Environmental degradation at Akwesasne took a quantum leap after the late 1950s when the St. Lawrence Seaway opened access to bountiful, cheap power. Access to power drew heavy industry that soon turned large segments of this magnificent river into open sewers.

Pollution in Iroquois country is not limited to Akwesasne, but it is most acute there. Onondaga Lake, for example, is so polluted that its fish are inedible. That lake, which once supplied the firekeepers of the Iroquois Confederacy with food, is today dominated by the skyline of Syracuse.

Onondaga Lake, the heart of the Onondaga nation and the Iroquois Confederacy, was said to be where Deganawidah, the great peacemaker, convinced Tadadaho to support the great peace. After many instances of chemical pollution in the lake, Onondaga is known as one of the most polluted bodies of water in the United States.

The pollution at Akwesasne (and at other points along the St. Lawrence River) is so widespread that it has affected the food chain into the Atlantic Ocean. Sea creatures feeding on fish from the St. Lawrence River, such as beluga whales, suffer from various forms of cancer, reproductive problems, and immune-system deficiencies. More than 500 environmental contaminants have been measured in autopsies of the wildlife in and near Akwesasne, 125 of them in the fish, with PCBs being only the most prominent.

TODAY'S TALENTS: AN ARRAY OF EXEMPLARY IROQUOIS PEOPLE

Despite acute environmental problems, the twenty-first century in Iroquois country has been a time of revival. The Iroquois, while contending with challenges to their sovereignty, environmental health, and land base, are a people with many diverse talents. The following biographical portraits provide brief sketches of people who engage in important issues for the Iroquois in the twenty-first century related to education, environment, and culture.

Ernest Benedict, Mohawk (1918–   ): Educator, Political Leader, and Spiritual Leader

Describing Mohawk Ernest Benedict in a few words is impossible because the range of his accomplishments is so broad. He has been a central figure in an effort that resulted in Native elders and spiritual leaders being recognized as equals of chaplains in Canadian prisons; he also helped win recognition and provision of Native religious ceremonies in the same prisons. He also has started Indian youth traditional dance and culture clubs that inspired young people to learn and practice their culture. Some of these students later worked with the North American Indian Travelling College and used their cultural knowledge to benefit others.

Benedict was the founder and longtime director of the Onake ("Birch Bark Canoe" in Mohawk) Corporation, which raises money for the benefit of other unincorporated community-based organizations and "canoes" the funds to them so that they will be able to carry on their work. At various times in his long life, Benedict has also been an athlete—a swimmer, skater, and long-distance runner—as well as a graceful traditional dancer.

As a political figure at Akwesasne, Benedict has served as an elected chief on the St. Regis Band Council, which is recognized by the State of New York, as well as the Mohawk Council of Akwesasne, the elected council recognized by the Canadian federal government. (Akwesasne spans the border, so it has an elective council on each side, as well as a traditional chiefs' council, the Mohawk Council of Chiefs.) He served on the Mohawk Council of Akwesasne for seven terms of office between 1956 and 1982. He was voted in as a chief of the Kawehnoke district, which is also known as Cornwall Island; he was elected by the council in his last term of office to serve as the head chief, a title now known as grand chief. Benedict is also a condoled life chief (*Rotinonkwiseres*) with the traditional community government, a predecessor of the Mohawk Nation Council of Chiefs.

John C. Mohawk, Seneca (1944–2006): Educator and Author

John C. Mohawk (*Sotisisowah*), a prominent Haudenosaunee scholar and activist, combined the roles and talents of university professor, elder statesman, historian, master storyteller, international negotiator, and cultural revivalist. Mohawk's longtime friend and former student Lori Taylor wrote in a personal e-mail a day after his death, "John Mohawk talked about himself as a person who bridged worlds. We need people who can bridge those worlds, and translate each to the other. This is precisely what drew me to study with him. [Mohawk] could explain the flow of world history, mediate violent battles, and still talk to his neighbors on the reservation about corn, beans, squash, and diabetes."

"John was the heart of the Native Studies program at the University of Buffalo," friend and university colleague Bruce Jackson said. "Other people taught it, but he was the one who always provided the focus, the compassion, and the guiding intelligence. In addition, the students really loved him."

Mohawk was best known outside New York State as an author. His histories ranged the world, combining Native American and European themes in *Utopian Legacies*, for example, in which he examined Western ideological thought as a provocation of political oppression. "Nazism was a revitalization movement, complete with its own vision of utopia, its rationalizations for conquest and plunder, and an ability to disarm ordinary people's sense of morality and to plunge an entire nation . . . into an orgy of violence and murder," Mohawk wrote in a wide-ranging historical account that analyzes why utopian dreams so often turn into searing, nasty realities.

John Kim Bell, Mohawk (1953–): Orchestra Conductor

John Kim Bell, composer, conductor, administrator, pianist, and mentor of many other musicians (including country star Shania Twain), was the first Native American to be employed as a professional orchestra conductor. Bell, who conducted with the National

Ballet of Canada, has also been guest conductor with London's Royal Philharmonic Orchestra

Bell was a conductor for several Broadway musicals during the late 1970s, including the international company of *A Chorus Line* (1978–1980). While conducting more than 30 American national tours and musicals, Bell worked with many notable people, including Lauren Bacall, Juliet Prowse, and Vincent Price. He served as conductor/pianist for *The Redd Foxx Show*, *The Sonny Bono Show*, and the Bee Gees. Bell also studied in Siena, Italy, with Franco Ferrara; he worked, as well, with the Dance Theatre of Harlem, the Eglevsky Ballet, and on several opera productions.

In 1980 and 1981, Bell served as apprentice conductor with Andrew Davis and the Toronto Symphony; he debuted as conductor on May 5, 1981. During 1984, Anthony Azzopardi produced a documentary biography describing Bell's musical career that was aired by the Canadian Broadcasting Corporation on October 8, 1984 (a video also was distributed by Kultur International). The show described a talented and passionate young man who broke social and racial barriers to fulfill a dream.

Bell inspired many Native Canadians. According to *The Encyclopedia of Music in Canada*, "Bell determined to devote his energies to the subject of education in the arts for Native peoples. He established in Toronto in 1985 the Canadian Native Arts Foundation (CNAF), to increase awareness of the artistic opportunities for, and to develop the potential talent of, the Native people through education." The foundation organizes benefit concerts to fund grants, scholarships, and tours for musicians of schools on Canadian Native reserves.

Charlie Hill, Oneida (1951–   ): Comedian

Charlie Hill, a nationally known comedian, who was raised on the Wisconsin Oneida reservation, honed his talents at the Comedy Shop in Los Angeles, which he calls "the fastest [comedy] track in the world." He has also performed in avant-garde theater in Seattle, New York, and other cities. Hill may be the most prominent contemporary Native American comedian, a master at stand-up improvisational humor with a biting ethnic wit who might remind listeners of Chris Rock crossed with Will Rogers.

Hill is Oneida, Mohawk, and Cree; growing up, he was exposed to the urban world of Detroit as well as the Wisconsin Oneida reservation; thus his humor has both rural and urban attributes, and appeals to a broad range of people. Hill's humor also has a national and a multiethnic character shaped, in part, by his residence as an adult, in New York City, Seattle, Sacramento, and Los Angeles, where he has been a regular performer at The Comedy Store. Hill has also made televised appearances with Richard Pryor, Johnny Carson, David Letterman, Jay Leno, and Rosanne Carter.

Hill's humor has a very serious political edge; he works to establish common interests between various indigenous peoples while tweaking everyone's nose. He observes in his comedy routine that European-American tourists who visit reservations often ask naive questions such as, "What Indian tribe was the fiercest?" or "Can I take your picture?" Hill exclaims, "We Indians ought to be tourists in the suburbs in a white neighborhood and see how they like it: 'Are you really white people? . . . Can I take your picture? How do you survive in these suburbs? My god!'"

G. Peter Jemison, Seneca (1945–   ): Artist

G. Peter Jemison, an eighth-generation descendant of Mary Jemison, is a Heron clan Seneca from Cattaraugus. An artist who formerly directed the American Indian Community House Gallery in New York City, Jemison has been the longtime manager of Ganondagan, a historic Seneca village site (designated as a state and federal historic site) 25 miles (40 kilometers) southeast of Rochester, New York. Jemison has also been active in national efforts to advocate the return of Native American remains and funerary objects from museums and other non-Indian archives.

Jemison has served as chairman of the Haudenosaunee Standing Committee on Burial Rules and Regulations. "What we see objectively is when you ask a museum like the New York State Museum what remains could be identified as Caucasian, that number is zero, or very close to zero," he has said. "When you ask about Native American [remains], that's all there is. Isn't there something strange about this?"

Jemison (whose media as an artist include acrylics, pen and ink, charcoal, and colored pencils) began to draw as a boy. Encouraged by his parents and art teachers, he studied art from 1962 to 1967 at the State University of New York at Buffalo. He also studied art at the University of Siena in Italy in 1964.

In addition to his reputation as an artist, Jemison is well known in Haudenosaunee country as an organizer of shows for other artists. One example of the many shows that Jemison has curated was "Where We Stand: Contemporary Haudenosaunee Artists," which was on exhibit from August 15 to December 21, 1997, at the New York State Historical Association Fenimore Art Museum. This show featured a number of Haudenosaunee artists active in a wide array of forms, from painting to basket weaving, silversmithing, prints, and sculpture.

Oren Lyons, Onondaga (1930–   ): Political Leader, Artist, Lacrosse Player, and Philosopher

Oren Lyons, whose Onondaga name is Joagquisho ("Bright Sun"), became known worldwide during the last half of the twentieth century as an author, publisher, and crisis negotiator, as well as a spokesman for the Haudenosaunee in several world forums. He is an accomplished graphic artist as well as a renowned lacrosse player and coach. Lyons's father also was a well-known goal-keeper. In 1990, Lyons organized an Iroquois national team that played in the World Lacrosse Championships in Australia. In addition, Lyons worked as a professor of Native American stud-ies at the State University of New York at Buffalo. Lyons also is known as an author, notably as lead author of *Exiled in the Land of the Free* (1992).

Born in 1930 and raised on reservations in New York, Oren Lyons became a national champion lacrosse player, a graphic designer, and an international activist for indigenous groups. *Above*, Lyons leads a protest in the basement of Capitol Plaza in Albany, New York.

Lyons has spoken before the United Nations General Assembly, and he used some of his time on one occasion to ask why the body had no seats for the bears and the eagles. He speaks for trees that cannot flee the chainsaw. He also speaks on behalf of salmon, herring, tuna, and haddock killed in their spawning beds by runoff from eroded hillsides. "We had alarming news from the Four Directions about fish, wildlife, and birds, contaminated, sick, and disappearing," Lyons told the author. "And today we continue to speak on their behalf. Today, they are more endangered than ever, and if anything, their conditions are worse. . . . As long as you make war against *Etenoha* (Mother Earth), there can never be peace."

Oren Lyons Speaks at the United Nations

Oren Lyons, a "faithkeeper" for the Grand Council, often represents the Iroquois at world forums, including the United Nations. He addressed that body on December 10, 1992, to mark the upcoming Year of Indigenous Peoples. He said, in part:

> The catastrophes that we have suffered at the hands of our brothers from across the seas [have] been unremitting and inexcusable. It has crushed our people, and our Nations, down through the centuries. You brought us disease and death and the idea of Christian dominion over heathens, pagans, savages. Our lands were declared "vacant" by Papal Bulls, which created law to justify the pillaging of our land.
>
> We were systematically stripped of our resources, religions, and dignity. Indeed, we became resources of labor for goldmines and canefields. Life for us was unspeakable, cruel. Our black and dark-skinned brothers and sisters were brought here from distant lands to share our misery and suffering and death. Yet we survived. I stand before you as a manifestation of the spirit of our people and our will to survive. The Wolf, our Spiritual Brother, stands beside us and we are alike in the Western mind: hated, admired, and still a mystery to you, and still undefeated.
>
> So then, what is the message I bring to you today? Is it our common future? It seems to me that we are living in a time of prophecy, a time of definitions and decisions. We are the generation with the responsibilities and the option to choose the Path of Life for the future of our children. Or the life and path which defies the Laws of Regeneration.
>
> Even though you and I are in different boats, you in your boat and we in our canoe, we share the same River of Life. What befalls me, befalls you. And downstream, downstream

(continues)

(continued)

in this River of Life, our children will pay for our selfishness, for our greed, and for our lack of vision.

Five hundred years ago, you came to our pristine lands of great forests, rolling plains, crystal clear lakes, and streams and rivers. And we have suffered in your quest for God, for Glory, for Gold. But, we have survived. Can we survive another 500 years of "sustainable development"? I don't think so. Not in the definitions that put "sustainable" in today. I don't think so.

So reality and the Natural Law will prevail; the Law of the Seed and Regeneration. We can still alter our course. It is *not* too late. We still have options. We need the courage to change our values to the regeneration of our families, the life that surrounds us. Given this opportunity, we can raise ourselves. We must join hands with the rest of Creation and speak of common sense, responsibility, brotherhood, and PEACE. We must understand that the law is the seed and only as true partners can we survive.

On behalf of the Indigenous People of the Great Turtle Island, I give my appreciation and thanks. *Dah ney' to*. Now I am finished.

Joanne Lynn Shenandoah (*Tekalihwa:khwa*), Oneida (1957–   ): Musician

In the early twenty-first century, Joanne Shenandoah, a Wolf Clan member of the Oneida Nation, had become a major presence in Native American folk music, fusing traditional Iroquois social songs with western music and other styles, including rock, techno, gospel, and folk. By 2008, her music had appeared on 14 individual recordings as well as 40 collections with other artists, including Neil Young and Bruce Cockburn.

Shenandoah's original compositions combined with her remarkable voice enable her to embellish the ancient songs of the Iroquois using a blend of traditional and contemporary

Award-winning musician Joanne Shenandoah is a prominent member of the Oneida nation and is known for blending traditional Native American music with other genres. She has performed at major national and international events, and is recognized as one of best-known contributors to Native American music.

instrumentation. According to *USA Today*: "The Native American music scene is brimming with skilled, adventurous artists, such as Robbie Robertson, Bill Miller, Rita Coolidge . . . and, arguably the best of all, the remarkable Joanne Shenandoah." Neil Young has said: "I consider the songs of Joanne Shenandoah the best tributes to Native American music." Shenandoah has won more Native American Music Awards than any other musician and has shared in a Grammy. In 2007, she was honored with a "Lifetime Achievement" award from the Native American Music Awards.

Shenandoah opened the 1994 concert at Woodstock before an audience of about 250,000 people. She also has appeared on stage at Carnegie Hall, the White House, and Kennedy Center, and during Earth Day on the Washington, D.C., Mall, and the Special Olympics.

Shenandoah contributed to an album in defense of activist Leonard Peltier and helped organize a concert of Native American women singers at the White House. Her music was featured in the Canadian Broadcasting Corporation's documentary *The War against the Indian* and in several local and national Public Broadcasting System documentaries in the United States. Shenandoah has sung around the world, from Australia (where she shared the stage with the Dalai Lama), to Spain, South Korea, Turkey, Belgium, and many other places.

Shenandoah also helped compose the musical score for the television series *Northern Exposure* and sang a song about the repatriation of Native American remains that was played four times during one segment of Cable News Network's *Larry King Live*. "Hopefully," Shenandoah said after the song was played on the talk show, "my listeners, Indian or not, can begin to see the human side of Indian problems."

At home, Shenandoah's family has been involved in a long-term dispute regarding abuse of Iroquois democratic traditions by "Nation Representative" Ray Halbritter, who has built extensive casino and business venues on New York Oneida land. The family believes that Halbritter took office as a nation leader without the consent of the people. Halbritter has retaliated by depriving the Shenandoahs and other protesters of services and membership in the Oneida Nation, as well as by ordering police to demolish some of their homes.

Chronology

Time Unknown	North America is created by sky beings on the back of a giant turtle. Human life begins in the midst of a struggle between good and evil.
circa 1000	Iroquoian peoples adapt agriculture by domesticating the "three sisters"—corn, beans, and squashes.
circa 1050–1150	The Haudenosaunee Confederacy is founded to unite strife-torn peoples in a century of epic debate and struggle.

Timeline

circa 1050–1150
The Haudenosaunee Confederacy is founded

1776
The American Revolution begins, splitting the Haudenosaunee Confederacy

1000 **1650**

circa 1000
Iroquoian peoples adapt agriculture

1534
Jacques Cartier first meets the Haudenosaunee

circa 1650
The Beaver Wars take place

1534, 1535, and 1541–1542   Jacques Cartier's voyages along the St. Lawrence River of Turtle Island (North America) are used by King Francis I of France to lay claim to large portions of northeastern North America.

1609, 1615   Samuel de Champlain, exploring for France, comes into contact with the Haudenosaunee in 1609. Champlain leads expeditions against the Haudenosaunee and allies with the Wyandot (Huron) in 1609 and 1615.

circa 1650   In the "Beaver Wars" the Haudenosaunee battle the Wyandot (Huron), culminating in their defeat and assimilation by the Haudenosaunee about 1650.

1742, 1744   Lancaster treaty councils; Canassatego advises English colonies to unite on an Iroquois model.

1754   Albany Congress; Benjamin Franklin proposes a plan for colonial union with Iroquois and British roots.

1779

General John Sullivan's raids destroy much of Seneca country

1784–1838

Many Haudenosaunee land holdings are taken through fraudulent treaty claims

1800   **1985**

circa 1800

Handsome Lake provides a code of conduct that is still widely followed

1959

The St. Lawrence Seaway opens; Iroquois country becomes the site of many polluting industrial plants

1985

In a Supreme Court ruling, the Oneida people win rights to 100,000 acres of land transferred to New York in 1795

1776 Onset of the American Revolution; the Haudenosaunee Confederacy splits.

1777–1778 The Oneida rescue George Washington's famished forces at Valley Forge with corn.

1779 General John Sullivan's raids destroy much of Seneca country, including 60 villages and their farm fields; the raids, ordered by George Washington as "chastisement" using "the rod or correction," are carried out with uncommon cruelty. Their economy destroyed, the Seneca suffer disease and hunger for years afterward.

1783 The Treaty of Paris formalizes United States independence and draws the border between the United States and Canada (which remains under British control) through Iroquois country without consulting the Iroquois Grand Council.

1784 The Fort Stanwix Treaty is negotiated, in which the United States initially proposes to expel Iroquois who had aided the British during the Revolutionary War. The Grand Council rejects the treaty. As finally negotiated, the treaty recognizes the Haudenosaunee's ownership of their aboriginal lands.

1794 The Canandaigua (Pickering) Treaty establishes a commission to formalize the border between the United States and Canada. Part of the treaty upholds the right of the Mohawk and other Haudenosaunee peoples to pass freely over the U.S.-Canadian border.

1784–1838 Many of the Haudenosaunee nations' land holdings are taken through fraudulent treaty claims; many of these are illegal because they violate the various nonintercourse acts passed by Congress during the same period. These acts require congressional approval of Indian land cessions to prevent fraud. As a result of these land cessions, many Haudenosaunee move to Canada (to Grand River and other communities), Wisconsin, Kansas, and Indian Territory (later Oklahoma). The Buffalo Creek Treaty of 1838 is one of the most worst government-assisted land frauds in United States history.

circa 1800 Even as the Iroquois lose much of their land, a revival movement begins in a religious context. The Seneca Handsome Lake provides a code of conduct that is still widely followed today.

Early 1920s The Cayuga Deskaheh (Levi General), Tadadaho (speaker) of the Iroquois Grand Council at Grand River, Ontario, asserts independence from Canadian jurisdiction. He travels to the headquarters of the League of Nations in Geneva, Switzerland, carrying a Haudenosaunee passport, with an appeal for support from the international community.

1959 The St. Lawrence Seaway opens; Iroquois (especially Seneca and Mohawk) country becomes the site of many polluting industrial plants; agriculture and fisheries are destroyed.

1965 The United States Army Corps of Engineers completes the Kinzua Dam, as its rising water inundates all of the Senecas' Cornplanter Grant.

1968, 1988 Because officials in Canada fail to observe the 1794 Canandaigua (Pickering) Treaty, the Akwesasne Mohawk (whose home straddles the border) blockade an international bridge in 1968. Akwesasne leader Mike Mitchell is arrested the same year for transporting a number of household goods across the border, a case that is revisited with another border crossing in 1988.

1985 In *County of Oneida v. Oneida Indian Nation*, the Oneida people win rights to 100,000 acres of land transferred to New York State in 1795, while George Washington was president of the United States.

1990s Widespread conflict (and sometimes fatal violence) over gambling racks Iroquois country.

1995 to date Conflict over leadership in Oneida country; Ray Halbritter opens the Turning Stone Casino and evicts traditional Oneida who oppose his government from their homes.

Glossary

Albany Congress of 1754   Colonial delegates met with the Iroquois on trade and other matters as Benjamin Franklin proposed a plan for union of the colonies that used some elements of the Iroquois system, as well as European political principles.

Beaver Wars   The Haudenosaunee (Iroquois) campaign against the Wyandot (Huron), which culminated in their defeat and assimilation by the Haudenosaunee about 1650.

"Bury the hatchet"   An Iroquois idiom that refers to the founding of the confederacy, as the member nations threw their weapons of war into a large pit under the Great Tree of Peace.

Canandaigua (Pickering) Treaty (1794)   Formalized the border between the United States and Canada. Part of the treaty upholds the right of the Mohawk and other Haudenosaunee peoples to pass freely between the two nations.

Clan mothers   Influential (often elderly) women in each clan who nominate male leaders for Iroquois governing councils.

Council of Matrons   Women's governing council that exercises influence on such policies as declarations of war by the male Grand Council.

Covenant Chain   Metaphor for alliance between the Iroquois and the British. In good times, this imaginary silver chain was said to be shining. In bad times, it had been tarnished.

Five Nations, Six Nations   The British term for the Haudenosaunee (Iroquois) Confederacy. The original five nations are the Mohawk, Oneida, Onondaga, Cayuga, and Seneca. The Tuscarora were adopted early during the eighteenth century as the sixth nation.

Grand Council   The central governing body of the Haudenosaunee Confederacy. The original Grand Council is located at Onondaga, south of Syracuse, New York; a second Grand Council was formed in Canada, at Grand River, Ontario, after the American Revolution.

Great Law of Peace   The Iroquois' "Great Binding Law" (*Kaianerekowa*), or constitution, outlining the government of the six nations.

Great White Pine   National symbol of the Haudenosaunee Confederacy, with an eagle flying overhead to protect the people from threats, and four White Roots extending to all directions to unite the Iroquois nations and other peoples. Weapons of war are to be buried under the roots of the tree.

Iroquois   French name for the Haudenosaunee.

Jigonsaseh   The position title of the Head Clan Mother of the Haudenosaunee League.

Lacrosse   Iroquois sport that inspired a similar game played by many people around the world today. Originally lacrosse, also called "The Little Brother of War," could be played across long distances.

Longhouse   1. Traditional Haudenosaunee dwelling, home to several extended families. 2. Symbol of the confederacy ("Haudenosaunee" means "People of the Longhouse.")

Matrilineal   A culture in which influence (and sometimes political appointments) follow the female line, such as the Iroquois; contrasts to patrilineal, in which influence follows male descent.

Removal   U.S. government policy by which Native Americans were forced from their homelands, mostly during the nineteenth century, and assigned other lands, often in Indian Territory (now Oklahoma). The Haudenosaunee fought Removal and usually prevailed, although some Iroquois moved to other places. An example is the Oneida of Wisconsin, who live near Green Bay.

"Sleep on it"   An idiom in English that comes directly from the debating practices of the Iroquois Grand Council, in which no important decision was made the same day it was introduced, to allow tempers to cool.

Tadadaho   Speaker of the Iroquois Confederacy.

Thanksgiving cycle   Yearlong series of Iroquois ceremonies associated with the changes in seasons, tying agriculture together with spirituality.

Wampum belts   A form of written communication that records important documents (such as the Great Law of Peace) and important events, such as treaties.

Bibliography

Akwesasne Notes, ed. *A Basic Call to Consciousness* [1978]. Rooseveltown, N.Y.: Akwesasne Notes, 1986.

Aldridge, Alfred O. "Franklin's Deistical Indians." *Proceedings of the American Philosophical Society* 44 (August, 1950): 398–410.

Anderson, Wallace (Mad Bear). "The Lost Brother: An Iroquois Prophecy of Serpents," in Shirley Hill Witt and Stan Steiner, eds. *The Way: An Anthology of American Indian Literature.* New York: Vintage, 1972, pp. 243–247.

Anthony, Susan B., Elizabeth Cady Stanton, and Matilda Joslyn Gage. *History of Woman Suffrage.* Salem, N.H.: Ayer Co., 1985.

Aquila, Richard. *The Iroquois Restoration: Iroquois Diplomacy on the Colonial Frontier, 1701–1754.* Detroit: Wayne State University Press, 1983.

Armstrong, William N. *Warrior in Two Camps: Ely S. Parker.* Syracuse, N.Y.: Syracuse University Press, 1978.

Biggar, H. P. *Works of Samuel de Champlain.* 7 vols. Toronto: The Champlain Society, 1922–1936.

Bilharz, Joy A. *The Allegany Senecas and Kinzua Dam: Forced Relocation through Two Generations.* Lincoln: University of Nebraska Press, 1998.

Bonvillain, Nancy. "Gender Relations in Native North America." *American Indian Culture and Research Journal* 13:2 (1989): 1–28.

———, ed. "Iroquoian Women." *Studies on Iroquoian Culture.* Occasional Publications in Northeastern Anthropology, No. 6. Rindge, N.H.: Department of Anthropology, Franklin Pierce College, 1980: 47–58.

Boorstin, Daniel J. *The Lost World of Thomas Jefferson.* New York: Henry Holt & Co., 1948.

Boyd, Julian. "Dr. Franklin, Friend of the Indian," in Ray Lokken Jr., ed. *Meet Dr. Franklin.* Philadelphia: Franklin Institute, 1981.

Brown, Judith K. "Economic Organization and the Position of Women Among the Iroquois." *Ethnohistory* 17:3/4 (Summer/Fall 1970): 151–167.

Child, Lydia Maria. *Hobomok and Other Writings on Indians,* ed. Carolyn L. Karcher. New Brunswick, N.J.: Rutgers University Press, 1986.

Colden, Cadwallader. *The History of the Five Indian Nations Depending on the Province of New-York in America* [1727 and 1747]. Ithaca, N.Y.: Cornell University Press, 1968.

Cook, Ramsay, ed. *The Voyages of Jacques Cartier.* Toronto: University of Toronto Press, 1993.

Dennis, Matthew. *Cultivating a Landscape of Peace: Iroquois-European Encounters in Seventeenth-Century America.* Ithaca, N.Y.: Cornell University Press, 1993.

Fenton, William N. *The Great Law and the Longhouse: A Political History of the Iroquois Confederacy.* Norman: University of Oklahoma Press, 1998.

———. "Seth Newhouse's [Dayodekane's] Traditional History and Constitution of the Iroquois Confederacy." *Proceedings of the American Philosophical Society* 93:2 (1949): 141–158.

Flexner, James Thomas. *Mohawk Baronet.* New York: Harper & Row, 1959.

Franklin, Benjamin. *The Autobiography of Benjamin Franklin*, ed. John Bigelow. Philadelphia: J. B. Lippincott, 1868.

Gage, Matilda Joslyn. *Woman, Church and State* [1893]. Watertown, Mass.: Peresphone Press, 1980.

Graymont, Barbara. *The Iroquois in the American Revolution.* Syracuse, N.Y.: Syracuse University Press, 1972.

Grinde, Donald A. Jr. and Bruce E. Johansen. *Exemplar of Liberty: Native America and the Evolution of Democracy.* Los Angeles: UCLA American Indian Studies Center, 1991.

Hamilton, Milton W. *Sir William Johnson: Colonial American, 1715–1763.* Port Washington, N.Y.: Kennikat Press, 1976.

Hauptman, Laurence M. *The Iroquois in the Civil War: From Battlefield to Reservation.* Syracuse, N.Y.: Syracuse University Press, 1993.

———. *The Iroquois Struggle for Survival: World War II to Red Power.* Syracuse, N.Y.: Syracuse University Press, 1986.

Heckewelder, John. *History, Manners, and Customs of the Indian Nations Who Once Inhabited Pennsylvania and the Neighboring States* [1820, 1876]. The First American Frontier Series. New York: Arno Press and The New York Times, 1971.

Hewitt, J[ohn] N[apoleon] B[rinton]. "A Constitutional League of Peace in the Stone Age of America: The League of the Iroquois and Its Constitution." *Smithsonian Institution Series* (1920): 527–545.

———. "Some Esoteric Aspects of the League of the Iroquois." *Proceedings of the International Congress of Americanists* 19 (1915): 322–326.

Jacobs, Renée. "Iroquois Great Law of Peace and the United States Constitution: How the Founding Fathers Ignored the Clan Mothers." *American Indian Law Review* 16:2 (1991): 497–531.

Jacobs, Wilbur R. "Wampum: The Protocol of Indian Diplomacy." *William and Mary Quarterly*, 3rd ser. 4:3 (October, 1949): 596–604.

Jacobs, Wilbur R. *Wilderness Politics and Indian Gifts*. Lincoln: University of Nebraska Press, 1966.

Jemison, Pete. "Mother of Nations—The Peace Queen, a Neglected Tradition." *Akwe:kon* (1988): 68–70.

Jennings, Francis. *The Ambiguous Iroquois Empire: The Covenant Chain Confederation of Indian Tribes with English Colonies from Its Beginnings to the Lancaster Treaty of 1744*. New York: W.W. Norton, 1984.

Jennings, Francis, ed.; William N. Fenton, joint ed.; Mary A. Druke, associate ed.; David R. Miller, research ed. *The History and Culture of Iroquois Diplomacy: An Interdisciplinary Guide to the Treaties of the Six Nations and Their League*. Syracuse, N.Y.: Syracuse University Press, 1985.

Johansen, Bruce E. *Forgotten Founders: Benjamin Franklin, The Iroquois and the Rationale for the American Revolution*. Ipswich, Mass.: Gambit, 1982.

Johansen, Bruce E., and Barbara Alice Mann. *Encyclopedia of the Haudenosaunee (Iroquois Confederacy)*. Westport, Conn.: Greenwood Press, 2000.

Johansen, Bruce E. Review, Joy Porter, "To Be Indian: The Life of Iroquois-Seneca Arthur Caswell Parker." *American Indian Culture and Research Journal* 26:3 (2002):167–168.

Johnson, Elias, Chief. *Legends, Traditions, and Laws of the Iroquois, or Six Nations* [1881]. New York: AMS Press, 1978.

Lipsyte, Robert. "Lacrosse: All-American Game." *New York Times Sunday Magazine*, June 15, 1986, 28.

Lyons, Oren, John Mohawk, Vine Deloria Jr., Laurence Hauptman, Howard Berman, Donald A. Grinde Jr., Curtis Berkey, and Robert Venables. *Exiled in the Land of the Free: Democracy, Indian Nations, and the Constitution*. Santa Fe, N.M.: Clear Light Publishers, 1992.

Lyons, Oren. Haudenosaunee Faithkeeper, Chief Oren Lyons addressing delegates to the United Nations Organization to open "The Year of the Indigenous Peoples" (1993) in the United Nations General Assembly Auditorium, United Nations Plaza, New York City, December 10, 1992. Accessed June 1, 2009. Available online. URL: http://www.ratical.org/many_worlds/6Nations/OLatUNin92.html.

Mann, Barbara A. "Haudenosaunee (Iroquois) Women, Legal and Political Status." *The Encyclopedia of Native American Legal Tradition.* Ed. Bruce Elliott Johansen. Westport, Conn.: Greenwood Press, 1998: 112–131.

————. *Iroquoian Women: Gantowisas of the Haudenosaunee League.* New York: Peter Lang Publishers, 2000.

————. "The Lynx in Time: Haudenosaunee Women's Traditions and History." *American Indian Quarterly.* 21:3 (1997): 423–450.

Mann, Barbara Alice. *George Washington's War on Native America.* Westport, Conn.: Praeger Publishers, 2005.

Mann, Barbara A. and Jerry L. Fields. "A Sign in the Sky: Dating the League of the Haudenosaunee." *American Indian Culture and Research Journal.* 21:2 (1997): 105–163.

Miller, David R., ed. *The History and Culture of Iroquois Diplomacy: An Interdisciplinary Guide to the Treaties of the Six Nations and Their League.* Syracuse, N.Y.: Syracuse University Press, 1985.

Mohawk, John. "Economic Motivations—An Iroquoian Perspective." *Northeast Indian Quarterly* 6 (1 & 2) Spring/Summer, 1989, 56–63.

Morgan, Lewis Henry. *League of the Haudenosaunee, or Iroquois* [1851]. 2 vols. New York: Burt Franklin, 1901.

Morison, Samuel Eliot. *Samuel de Champlain: Father of New France.* Boston: Little, Brown, 1972.

Mt. Pleasant, Jane. "The Iroquois Sustainers: Practices of a Long-term Agriculture in the Northeast." *Northeast Indian Quarterly* 6 (1&2) Spring/Summer, 1989, 33–39.

Nabokov, Peter. *Native Testimony.* New York: Viking, 1991.

Parker, Arthur. *The History of The Seneca Indians* [1926]. Port Washington, N.Y.: Ira J. Friedman, 1967.

————. *The Constitution of the Five Nations, or The Iroquois Book of the Great Law.* Albany: University of the State of New York, 1916.

————. *Iroquois Uses of Maize and Other Food Plants.* Albany: University of the State of New York, 1910.

————. *The Life of General Ely S. Parker, Last Grand Sachem of the Iroquois and General Grant's Military Secretary.* Buffalo, N.Y.: Buffalo Historical Society, 1919.

————. *Parker on the Iroquois.* Ed. William N. Fenton. Syracuse, N.Y.: Syracuse University Press, 1968.

————. *Seneca Myths and Folk Tales.* Intro. William N. Fenton. Lincoln: University of Nebraska Press, 1989.

————. *The White Roots of Peace.* Empire State Historical Publication Series No. 56. Port Washington, N.Y.: Ira J. Friedman, 1946.

————. [*Gawaso Wanneh*]. *The Code of Handsome Lake, the Seneca Prophet.* New York State Museum Bulletin 163, Education Department Bulletin No. 530, November 1, 1912. Albany: University of the State of New York, 1913.

————. *Notes on the Ancestry of Cornplanter.* Rochester, N.Y.: Lewis H. Morgan Chapter, 1927.

Porter, Joy. *To Be Indian: The Life of Iroquois-Seneca Arthur Caswell Parker.* Norman: University of Oklahoma Press, 2001.

Price, Darby Li Po. "Laughing Without Reservation: Indian Standup Comedians." *American Indian Culture and Research Journal* 22:4 (1998): 255–271.

Quintana, Jorge. "Agricultural Survey of New York State Iroquois Reservations, 1990." *Northeast Indian Quarterly* 8:1 (Spring, 1991): 32–36.

Reaman, G. Elmore. *The Trail of the Iroquois Indians: How the Iroquois Nation Saved Canada for the British Empire.* London: Frederick Muller, 1967.

Richter, Daniel K. and James H. Merrell, eds. *Beyond the Covenant Chain: The Iroquois and Their Neighbors in Indian North America, 1600–1800.* Syracuse, N.Y.: Syracuse University Press, 1987.

Rosier, Paul C. *Serving Their Country: American Indian Politics and Patriotism in the Twentieth Century.* Cambridge, Mass.: Harvard University Press, 2009.

Stokes, John. *Thanksgiving Address: Greetings to the Natural World.* Tracking Project, Six Nations Indian Museum, 1996.

Sullivan, James, ed. *The Papers of Sir William Johnson.* Albany, N.Y.: University of the State of New York, 1921–1965.

Thomas, Chief Jacob [Cayuga], with Terry Boyle. *Teachings from the Longhouse.* Toronto: Stoddart Publishing, 1994.

Tooker, Elisabeth. "The League of the Iroquois: Its History, Politics, and Ritual." *Handbook of North American Indians, Northeast* (Vol. 15). Washington, D.C.: Smithsonian Institution, 1978, 418–441.

————, ed. *Native North American Spirituality of the Eastern Woodlands: Sacred Myths, Dreams, Visions, Speeches, Healing Formulas, Rituals, and Ceremonials.* New York: Paulist Press, 1979.

Vecsey, Christopher, and William A. Starna, eds. *Iroquois Land Claims.* Syracuse, N.Y.: Syracuse University Press, 1988.

Venables, Robert W. "The Founding Fathers: Choosing to Be Romans." *Northeast Indian Quarterly* 6:4 (Winter, 1989): 30-35.

———. "More Than a Game." *Northeast Indian Quarterly* 6:3 (Fall, 1989): 12–15.

Vennum, Thomas. *American Indian Lacrosse: Little Brother of War.* Washington, D.C.: Smithsonian Institution Press, 1994.

Wagner, Sally Roesch. *The Untold Story of the Iroquois Influence on Early Feminists.* Aberdeen, S.D.: Sky Carrier Press, 1996.

———. "The Iroquois Confederacy: A Native American Model for Non-sexist Men," *Changing Men,* (Spring–Summer, 1988): 32–33.

Wallace, Anthony F. C. *The Death and Rebirth of the Seneca.* New York: Knopf, 1970.

———. "Political Organization and Land Tenure Among the Northeastern Indians, 1600–1830." *Southwestern Journal of Anthropology* 13(1957): 301–321.

Wallace, Paul A. W. *The White Roots of Peace.* Philadelphia: University of Pennsylvania Press, 1946.

Waugh, F. W. *Iroquois Foods and Preparation* [1916]. Ottawa: National Museum of Canada, 1973.

White Roots of Peace. *The Great Law of the Longhouse People.* Rooseveltown, N.Y.: Akwesasne Notes, 1977.

Wilson, Edmund. *Apologies to the Iroquois.* New York: Vintage Books, 1960.

Woodbury, Hanni, comp. *Concerning the League: The Iroquois League Tradition as Dictated in Onondaga by John Arthur Gibson,* comp. Hanni Woodbury, Reg Henry, and Harry Webster on the basis of A. A. Goldenweiser's manuscript. Algonquian and Iroquoian Linguistics, Memoir No. 9. Winnipeg, Manitoba: University of Manitoba Press, 1992.

Further Resources

Allen, Paula Gunn. *The Sacred Hoop: Recovering the Feminine in American Indian Traditions.* Boston: Beacon Press, 1986.

Cronon, William. *Changes in the Land: Indians, Colonists, and the Ecology of New England.* New York: Hill and Wang, 1983.

DeVoto, Bernard. *The Course of Empire.* Boston: Houghton-Mifflin, 1952.

Eccles, William John. *The Canadian Frontier, 1534–1760* [1969]. Albuquerque: University of New Mexico Press, 1983.

Hauptman, Laurence M. *The Iroquois Struggle for Survival: World War II to Red Power.* Syracuse, N.Y.: Syracuse University Press, 1986.

Johansen, Bruce E., and Barbara Alice Mann. *Encyclopedia of the Haudenosaunee (Iroquois Confederacy).* Westport, Conn.: Greenwood Press, 2000.

Mohawk, John C. *Utopian Legacies: A History of Conquest and Oppression in the Western World.* Santa Fe, N.M.: Clear Light Publishers, 2000.

Nabokov, Peter. *Native Testimony.* New York: Viking, 1991.

Sword, Wiley. *President Washington's Indian War: The Struggle for the Old Northwest, 1790–1795.* Norman: University of Oklahoma Press, 1985.

Trigger, Bruce G. *Children of the Aataentsic: A History of the Huron People.* Montreal: McGill-Queen's University Press, 1976.

———. *Natives and Newcomers: Canada's "Heroic Age" Reconsidered.* Kingston and Montreal: McGill-Queen's University Press, 1985.

Wallace, Paul A. W. *Indians in Pennsylvania.* Harrisburg: Pennsylvania Historical and Museum Commission, 1961.

Waters, Frank. *Brave Are My People.* Santa Fe, N.M.: Clear Light Publishers, 1992.

Web sites

Iroquois History

http://tolatsga.org/iro.html

This site has comprehensive information about the Iroquois, including details about the culture, population, history, and links to other nations.

Iroquois Indian Museum

http://www.iroquoismuseum.org/index.html

Located in New York, this educational institution is dedicated to foster-ing the understanding of the Iroquois people and promoting Iroquois art and artists. This multimedia site provides full-color photographs, student educational kits, genealogy information, a calendar of events, and links to other resources.

National Museum of the American Indian

http://www.nmai.si.edu

Established by an act of Congress in 1989, this Smithsonian museum works with Native people to educate the public about the cultures, tradi-tions, and beliefs of the indigenous people of the Western Hemisphere. The site also includes information on student programs, teacher lesson plans, and family programs.

Samuel de Champlain

http://www.samueldechamplain.com/

The biography of the French navigator, one of the first Europeans to come into contact with the Iroquois.

The Six Nations

http://www.ratical.org/many_worlds/6Nations/

Interviews, book excerpts, photographs, and links to other sites of interest make this site a good resource for information on the Six Nations.

Picture Credits

Index

About the Contributors

Author **BRUCE E. JOHANSEN** is a Professor of Communication and Native American Studies at the University of Nebraska at Omaha. He has written 33 books as of 2010. Johansen's first academic specialty was the influence of Native American political systems on United States political and legal institutions; his best-known books in this area are *Forgotten Founders* (1982) and *Exemplar of Liberty* (with Donald A. Grinde Jr.), published in 1991. Johansen also writes frequently about environmental subjects, including *The Encyclopedia of Global Warming Science and Technology* (2 vols., 2009), *Global Warming in the 21st Century* (3 vols., 2006), and *The Dirty Dozen: Toxic Chemicals and the Earth's Future* (2003).

Series editor **PAUL C. ROSIER** received his Ph.D. in American History from the University of Rochester in 1998. Dr. Rosier currently serves as Associate Professor of History at Villanova University (Villanova, Pennsylvania), where he teaches Native American History, American Environmental History, Global Environmental Justice Movements, History of American Capitalism, and World History.

In 2001 the University of Nebraska Press published his first book, *Rebirth of the Blackfeet Nation, 1912–1954*; in 2003, Greenwood Press published *Native American Issues* as part of its Contemporary Ethnic American Issues series. In 2006 he co-edited an international volume called *Echoes from the Poisoned Well: Global Memories of Environmental Injustice*. Dr. Rosier has also published articles in the *American Indian Culture and Research Journal*, the *Journal of American Ethnic History*, and *The Journal of American History*. His *Journal of American History* article, entitled "'They Are Ancestral Homelands: Race, Place, and Politics in Cold War Native America, 1945–1961," was selected for inclusion in *The Ten Best History Essays of 2006–2007*, published by Palgrave MacMillan in 2008; and it won the Western History Association's 2007 Arrell Gibson Award for Best Essay on the history of Native Americans. In 2009 Harvard University Press published his latest book, *Serving Their Country: American Indian Politics and Patriotism in the Twentieth Century*.